From a Town on the Hudson

From a Town *on the Hudson*

A Japanese Woman's Life in America

Yuko Koyano

TUTTLE
Signature
EDITIONS

TUTTLE SIGNATURE EDITIONS
2-6, Suido 1-chome, Bunkyo-ku, Tokyo 112, Japan

© 1996 by Yuko Koyano

LCC Card No. 96-60249
ISBN 0-8048-2092-9

First edition, 1996

Printed in Japan

To
Jane and Gene Holben
my host family of twenty-two years

Contents

 *Preface*

I AM SLIGHTLY hesitant to write about the beginning of my life because the place and the time in which I was born have made me feel a sense of guilt about the war.

I was born in China in 1946 as the fifth child of my parents. My father was a seaman and worked for a steamship company in Manchuria. The year I was born was a time of confusion and great scarcity of food after the war. I was a dying eight-month-old baby, just skin and bones, when my family returned to Japan in 1947. A cup of thin rice gruel my grandmother gave me saved my life. Until I was nine years old, I was weak and had a poor appetite, so I am small even today. I have not visited my birthplace since returning to Japan. Although the fact that Japan colonized China during the war makes me feel a sense of guilt, I long to see the beautiful city of Dalian.

I grew up in my father's hometown in Saga Prefecture, in the northern part of Kyushu. For family reasons, I moved to Chiba Prefecture in 1960 and then to Hyogo Prefecture in 1965. From 1965 to 1967, I studied English

literature at a women's college in Kyoto. Following graduation, I worked for an insurance company in Kobe for
about three years and then returned to Chiba Prefecture
to get married to an old high-school classmate, Toshio Koyano, in 1970.

I gave birth to our first boy in 1971. My husband, who
worked for a bank, passed the bank's test to go abroad for
study in 1972, and entered the graduate program of the
Wharton School at the University of Pennsylvania in 1973.

In 1974, our son, almost three then, and I joined my
husband, who lived on campus. This was the first time
for me to see America. Even though it was only a one-year
stay, I met many fine Americans. Mr. and Mrs. Holben,
among them, have been our host family in the United
States since then. In 1975, we returned to Japan and
learned that my father, sixty-one, had died seven days earlier. We resumed our life in Japan in one of the company's
apartment houses in Tokyo. On Christmas Eve of 1976, I
gave birth to our second boy.

In 1985, my husband was transferred to New York on
business, and our family moved to the United States again,
to live in Fort Lee, New Jersey. This was our second
time in America. I had a problem with the language but
no culture shock. The abundance of nature there fascinated me, the spaciousness gave me a feeling of relief, and
American hospitality awakened something in me. I felt
refreshed in everything I did, as if America had infused
me with new life. If I could have spoken English fluently,
I would have talked enthusiastically about both the
United States and Japan to my American friends every

day. As it was, however, I kept my thoughts and feelings to myself.

When I realized how little ordinary Americans knew of Japan and what negative, stereotypical images of Japanese most Americans had, I thought that even with my poor English I would at least try to convey my feelings to my friends. I had one more way of expressing my feelings: writing. I wrote a booklet titled "My Memories" to show my gratitude to my friends and sent it to them right before I left the United States in 1990. That booklet became the basis for the essays in this present volume.

After I returned to Japan, I wanted to write about more of my experience in the United States. In the fall of 1991, I took a creative writing class at Tokyo's Asahi Culture Center to learn writing techniques. However, my mother, who had been waiting for me to come back to Japan, became ill and bedridden. I couldn't attend all the classes, but it was wonderful to learn more about writing. My mother died in 1992, and in the summer of 1993, I resumed my writing. The next year, my father-in-law, who had been the center of the family, also died. For these reasons, therefore, it took me some time to complete these thirty essays.

I believe that my friendships with Americans kept encouraging me to write. Moreover, I have received much encouragement from my husband, who gave me the chance to see America twice, and from our two sons, who gave me many opportunities to be a happy mother in the United States. I must express my affection and gratitude to them.

I offer my heartfelt thanks to Ms. Heidi Frank and Mr.

Bennett Walker, teachers at Margaret's Institute of Language in Funabashi City, Chiba Prefecture. Without their careful grammatical review, my readers wouldn't be able to accurately understand what I want to express.

I loved America and realized a greater love for Japan through this experience.

From a Town on the Hudson

1 *My Respected Professor*

THIS FIRST chapter does not have to do with my life in America but with my decision to write about it. I was motivated by my enormous admiration for a professor who taught me English literature at a women's university in Kyoto from 1965 to 1967.

Because the thirty-four-year-old gentleman at that time was witty, earnest, and attractive, he got the enthusiastic support of his young students. Even when his classes were over, nobody would let him go. We used to catch him on the bench in front of the fountain on the college grounds, at a nearby temple, and sometimes at the faculty office. Not only did we meet him on campus, but one day in the fall ten students visited him at his home in Fushimi in the southern part of Kyoto. I remember our sitting close to one another in the narrow living room with his lovely wife and two children. Moreover, several students even visited his parents' home in Shimane Prefecture during the summer vacation. Each time we talked about English literature with the professor, I felt as if I could easily master the English language, create poems in English, and even write long stories in English. His ardent passion for English literature told us how worthwhile learning English was. He was such a vigorous and great teacher to us all and always treated everyone with the same consideration.

One warm June evening, however, at a streetcar station called Higashiyama Shichijo near the university, I happened to meet him on the way home. Hanging on to a strap in the rattling streetcar I was lucky enough to be given a private lecture about Shakespeare's *Macbeth*. But I couldn't concentrate on the lecture at all, because I was so excited by the unexpected encounter. While walking to the Kyoto Station terminal building after we had gotten off the streetcar, and before I said good-bye to him at the main wicket, I was just thinking how jealous my classmates would be of me the next day when they heard that I had had our favorite professor all to myself. I recall that I jumped with joy and almost whistled as I bounded up the steps to the platform for Osaka. The next day I was actually shunned by a jealous classmate, the first person I had told of my "betrayal."

The last time I saw the professor was at Kyoto Station in the summer of 1968, when he left for England to study at Oxford University. I had nothing to do with English for many years after that. I got married and enjoyed making a home and raising two sons. I even forgot how to spell "Saturday" or "January." When our younger son entered nursery school, I began to think about what I, as a person, liked most all my life. It was English. The words of that professor, who died of cancer in 1975 at the age of forty-four, rang in my mind. I felt that his humorous, wise, high-spirited, and warm-hearted style which he had shown us students was about to lead the way to my learning English again.

② *Moving to the United States*

"NO, I WON'T go to America." At the end of January 1985, the story opened with our sons' refusal to be transferred with their father's job to New York the coming spring. They said that they could live with their grandparents in Japan. The two boys' reaction was unexpected. However, it was impossible for us to leave our thirteen- and eight-year-old sons in Japan. Although we were living in what was soon to be the twenty-first century, when the techniques of broadcasting had greatly improved, we still couldn't see what the real world was like as long as we stayed in Japan. This would be a chance for our school-age boys to see the world outside of Japan. My husband and I insisted that our family should live together even though we would be living abroad, and we told the boys that we would like to have a new life together in the United States. Then the two brothers seemed to reconsider the move and forgot to fight with each other for a few days. They still seemed to be worrying about their pet lovebirds and goldfish, but they agreed with us in the end.

"Mother, do you understand English?" Actually, I had majored in English. Besides that, I had had the experience of living abroad: I had been in Philadelphia in 1974 with my husband when he was studying at the Wharton School. Nevertheless, I couldn't be confident about English. In Philadelphia, I could neither catch what Americans said nor make myself understood in English very well. I remembered regretting that I was unable to express what I thought. This would be my second time in America and, besides that, our sons were growing. I didn't have to look after my family all day. This would be an occasion for me to master spoken English. I was optimistic. In January 1985, I never imagined that I would return to Japan in 1990 still being unable to speak English well.

"What school will I go to?" "Will I be able to speak English soon?" "Are the American teachers friendly?" "What kind of lunch will I eat at an American school?" "Will you really help me if I have trouble?" "What do American boys do for fun?" Both of our sons worried about what they would undergo in the United States. As parents, we naturally would help them whenever they needed it. My husband and I tried to alleviate their fears as much as possible. If the new experiences in the United States could become a positive part of their lives, that would be wonderful. For the younger son, who was born in 1976, it would be the first time to live in America. In reality, especially in the beginning, they struggled with many things in their American schools that they had been anxious about. However, both of my sons were helped by many Americans and were able to overcome their difficulties.

"I want a wife, too!" I ridiculously said to myself, counting the number of sealed boxes in our house. From February to the end of March in 1985, I was occupied with packing, doing daily household chores, looking after my children, and taking care of every other kind of preparation. But I couldn't drop my routine household chores and taking care of my children. My husband also was busy handing over his job at the bank and preparing for departure earlier than the rest of us. However, thanks to his wife, delicious meals and a Japanese-style deep bath filled with comfortably heated water were always guaranteed to be waiting for him at home. Even though I was pleased when he told me that he was happy, I was still busy. Our older son was no help because he was occupied with his tennis club activities at his junior high school until it got dark. In addition to packing, I had a gardener trim the trees as much as possible, called a secondhand bookseller, and disposed of unused articles. To prepare for renting our house to the bank my husband worked for, I also asked a housing company to check the boiler and the roof. In addition, I often took our younger son to the doctor's office, went shopping, cooked meals, washed clothes, hung them out to dry and, in the afternoon, took them in and prepared the bath as usual. I attended several farewell parties, too. After my husband had left for New York in the middle of March, I at last invited some people to our house. My mother-in-law, sixty-four then, came to help me and stayed at our house for a while. My mother, seventy then, also came but soon returned home to Yokohama because the mere sight of the chaotic rooms seemed to exhaust her. Moving was really a big job. Unlike endless housework, however, it had an ending. I, thirty-eight then, was losing weight.

"See you again!" "Have a safe trip!" "Come back as soon as possible!" On April 13th, our two sons and I arrived at John F. Kennedy Airport in New York and met my husband, who had arrived a month earlier. It was cold and the sky was gloomy-looking. We got into a limousine and headed for Fort Lee, New Jersey. Listening to my husband's description of our new home, town, schools, and car, all of which he had arranged for us, I saw forsythia blooming along the highway. It looked like a light in a gray world on our family's first day in the United States of America.

③ *Schools of Their Own Choice*

"WHAT SCHOOL will I go to?" both of our sons asked us almost every thirty minutes after arriving in New York. For all of us, that was a big problem. About the schools, there were a few choices we would be able to make: a public school, a private Catholic school, or a Japanese school in New York. For the older son, my husband and I had thought it might be better for him to transfer to the Japanese school so he would not have to struggle with the language problem. For the younger son, the choices were limited to two schools: a private Catholic school or a public school. The Japanese school did not include the lower elementary grades at that time, and he would have been in the third grade if he had been in Japan. We agreed that we would decide after checking on those schools.

About 8:30 A.M., April 15, 1985, two days after we arrived at our new residence in Fort Lee, my husband, who had arrived a month earlier, took us to those three schools. Both Fort Lee School #3 and Holy Trinity School were on Myrtle Avenue, in the neighborhood where we lived. We first went to the Holy Trinity School. It was a small, pretty school. Students wearing school uniforms gathered in the school yard around their principal, a woman. Then they entered the classrooms for the first period of the day. We went to the school office and waited until the principal came. The secretary gave us a kind look and said, "You don't have to be nervous" to our two sons, who had been taken to an unknown world. Soon the principal came into the office. After we greeted each other, she told us about the school. Because there wasn't room for our sons in the school at that time, she said that she couldn't enroll them. "However," she continued, "if you will come again in September, I will be able to welcome your sons."

Then we went to Public School #3. The secretary was a beautiful, friendly-looking lady. She was busy with one job after another, but she told us that our younger son could enter any time with the completed health forms and a certificate of proof that he had attended a Japanese elementary school. That was all. It didn't take even one minute. To many Japanese parents who had been accustomed to Japan's bureaucratic system, this might have been the very first moment when they noticed how open the school system of the United States is. We also knew many Japanese students were in the school. This seemed to be the most important thing for our younger son.

Then, because we had no car yet, we walked to the bus stop at the George Washington Bridge and got on a bus going over to the New York side. There we took subways and buses and then walked to the Japanese school. "It's too far." This was the first impression that we had as we made our way there. We heard an explanation about the school and that our older son would be able to transfer to the school.

We returned to Fort Lee and then went to the Lewis F. Cole Middle School. There were no students around since the school-day was over, and we felt assured by the open atmosphere of the school. A secretary at the office looked kind, and she explained a little about the school, just as the secretary of School #3 had done that morning. Our older son could be accepted any day after submitting a health report.

Each school had its good points. However, as we couldn't wait until September, we gave up the idea of going to Holy Trinity School. This meant the younger son would go to School #3. That night we talked about the schools that we had visited during the day. As parents, my husband and I decided it would be best for our sons to choose their own schools. We weren't being irresponsible; we hoped that the boys would become people who could take responsibility for making their own decisions. That night was the very first time for our two sons to make an important decision concerning their new lives in the

United States. After a while, they said that they liked the public schools.

4 *The First Two Months*

MY SONS chose the public schools in the town where we lived. For them, the two months from April 18th to the end of the 1984–85 school year seemed to be an exciting as well as tense time.

Because my older son, Kyosuke, who was thirteen years old at the time, had been in Philadelphia when he was three years old, and also because there were few strict rules in his new school, Lewis F. Cole Middle School, he looked more relaxed there than in Japan's public junior high school. Besides, in the United States he had no daily piano practice and was not busy with after-school activities. He seemed to enjoy his free time fully. Though he couldn't speak English, he didn't seem to feel so anxious about it. The school had a bilingual class where he could learn American history and science in both English and Japanese. It seemed to be a surprising experience for him to be able to take lessons in fluent Japanese from an American teacher, Mrs. Wheeler. She also used to talk about Japan because she had been there. He was able to take the school trip to Washington, D.C., about ten days after he landed in the United States because of the teacher's timely advice, as well. Moreover, in his class, there were many Japanese girls but only one boy, who had come the previous year. Luckily he and my son became good friends immediately. Not only the students but also their parents could ask the teacher anything in Japanese. In a sense, the class was like a window through which Japanese newcomers could see the United States and Japan. Mrs. Wheeler always opened it wide with a smile.

My son was a member of the E.S.L.* class, as well. The class consisted of new students who came from several non-English-speaking countries. This was one of the amazing aspects of the United States, a country of immigrants. Even though the E.S.L. teacher, Mrs. Costantino, taught proper English words, my son learned English taboo words which were frequently used by American boys in the school sooner than he learned the lessons in the E.S.L. textbook. The worse the phrase was, the easier the new students seemed to pronounce it. My two sons exchanged the newly learned phrases including the accompanying gestures every day at home. I told them not to learn those bad words so eagerly, but I carefully listened to and memorized them. Especially when there were traffic jams, it was helpful for me to understand Americans who were yelling at each other. In other regular middle school classes, my son seemed to enjoy observing everything. It was pleasant for me to hear about it from him while we had supper together. During the first two months in the school, the eyes of my older son were opened to the world—the world outside of Japan.

* English as a Second Language.

From the first day, however, my younger son, Masahito, eight years old then, was in a situation that was different from his brother's. At 8:30 A.M., April 18th, 1985, in the office of School #3 he waited for his new homeroom teacher to come to pick him up. The secretary, Mrs. Makroulakis, kindly offered to take care of him and I left him there, looking as timid as if he were going to be kidnapped. Since we had just moved into our new home five days earlier, I was busy all day unpacking the many boxes we had sent from Japan. Before three o'clock, I went to pick him up at school. Many mothers were waiting at the gate for their children to come out of the school building. After a few minutes, I saw my son coming with a friendly lady who looked like a teacher. She was holding my son's hand. He looked tired and still nervous. I greeted the lady. She responded with *"Konnichiwa!,"* introduced herself as my son's homeroom teacher, and explained some rules of the school, school hours, how to order lunch, and so on. Her name was Mrs. Benedict, and she told me that my son said he didn't like American school. "However," she continued with her face beaming, "don't worry. Most of the new pupils say that in the beginning, but time opens their minds. Your son will be all right, too." I have forgotten what the weather was like that day, yet her sympathetic manner, like the warm sunlight of spring, certainly put me at ease. My son was in Mrs. Benedict's class for only two months until the school year ended in June. He, too, automatically became a member of the bilingual class as well as the E.S.L. class but couldn't explain what the classes were like as exactly as his older brother did.

I got to know the classes and the teachers, Mrs. Hishi-kawa and Mrs. Amato, when the parent–teacher confer-ence was held. In the bilingual class, my son seemed to prefer to take a rest as Mrs. Hishikawa, who was married to a Japanese gentleman and had raised their four chil-dren in Japan, understood how new pupils felt stress. In other classes, my younger son seemed to spend most of the school hours observing his new surroundings and es-pecially enjoying the snack time for kindergarten through second grade. Having a snack between classes was some-thing that never happened in Japan's elementary schools. He acquired a taste for American snacks such as Fruit Roll-Ups. The class he could participate in with confidence seemed to be math class. He certainly knew numbers, but it should have been impossible for him to understand the meaning of the problems written in English. When I saw his math textbook and the tests that he brought home, however, I realized why he could solve the problems. I found marks such as +, −, and × below each problem. Mrs. Benedict marked them for him so that he could dis-tinguish the addition, subtraction, and multiplication problems from one another. He looked happy showing me the results of his math test, but because of the help he received, he didn't get a grade on his report card for this marking period. One day in the middle of June, he told me immediately upon coming home from school about the "show and tell" class. His face lit up when he told about how he had tried to do his best when speaking his first English sentence: "This is a game-watch." I was sure that Mrs. Benedict had applauded for him. He added, "All the class applauded for me, too." The most important thing he learned about in the first two months may have been the American hospitality that his teacher showed.

Sumito Tachikawa and Kimigayo

THE SINGER wasn't applauded at that time because he sang the Japanese National Anthem, "Kimigayo," at the opening ceremony of the official tour of Japan's national sport to the United States. However, I thought he was a professional worthy of being praised.

At 7:30 P.M., Saturday, June 15th, 1985, the seats of Madison Square Garden were filled. The opening ceremony for the second day of the three-day grand sumo tournament in New York had begun. Everyone rose. As soon as the first part of Japan's "Kimigayo" sounded, the noise of the crowd in the large hall ebbed away. I recognized the voice of popular baritone singer Sumito Tachikawa. He looked very neat in a formal, black Japanese kimono and was singing near the *dohyo* (the raised sand-and-clay ring where sumo wrestlers fight) in the center of the pit. The middle-aged singer, who stood erect, seemed to overwhelm the tens of thousands of spectators with his sonorous voice before his appearance attracted their attention. The song affected me strongly at once. I wondered if it was nostalgia, but it seemed different. The stillness of the hall as well seemed distinguished from a mere sense of respect for the national anthem. Everybody seemed to be listening to him intently. A solemn feeling spread through the large sports arena and the song stood out in the hushed silence. "Is this really 'Kimigayo'?" I gazed, enraptured by the scene. To me, for many years this song had seemed different than it was today. The tempo had been as slow as the plodding of an ox, the melody as monotonous as a blowing siren, the words as tranquil as a lullaby. It had always been a dull chorus, besides. What's more, in Japan the song used to give rise to criticism among leftist circles because it hadn't been made the official anthem by the Constitution. So I never fully appreciated it in the right way. Tachikawa, however, successfully showed the charm of the song: His rich voice set off the gentle tempo, making the melody mysterious but graceful. The words were particularly peaceful: "May the reign of the Emperor continue for a thousand, nay, eight thousand generations and for the eternity that it takes for small pebbles to grow into a great rock and become covered with moss."* Unexpectedly, an image of the seahorse-shaped Japanese archipelago across the blue Pacific Ocean flashed into my mind. It was my homeland, lush and green. Because of this song, a feeling of pride that I was from Japan formed in my mind for the first time. I found myself a Tachikawa fan by the time the male American vocalist finished singing the bright "Star-Spangled Banner."

* *Nippon: The Land and Its People.* Nippon Steel Corporation, Personnel Development Division. Tokyo, 1984.

The tension in the hall was relieved as people burst out talking again, in anticipation of seeing Japanese sumo. Breathing in the sweet smell of popcorn, I looked forward to going to see a Tachikawa show after I returned to Japan. Six months later, however, the vocalist suddenly died of a brain hemorrhage in Japan. He was fifty-six. When I heard the news in the United States, I realized that I had been able to see only his back when he had so majestically sung "Kimigayo" at Madison Square Garden.

6 *Encounter with Sumo Wrestlers*

FOR AN AMERICAN audience, the parade of forty bare-foot wrestlers at the *dohyoiri** ritual seemed significant in the sense that they saw Japanese who were different from a group of Japanese businessmen wearing suits and glasses in Manhattan. The audience shouted with joy—as if anthropologists had finally discovered a primitive Japanese man. Everybody looked wide-eyed at the extraordinary, ancient-looking wrestlers and welcomed them with applause. The bulky wrestlers were dressed in colorfully embroidered *keshyo-mawashi* † and all wore the same distinctive hairstyles. They moved slowly in single file and performed their mysterious ring-entrance rite on the *dohyo*.

* Entrance to the *dohyo*.
† Ornamental apron worn by sumo wrestlers.

To tell the truth, I had never appreciated their old-fashioned appearance while I had lived in Japan. When I was small, I even mistook sumo wrestlers for big, tough women. The dour expressions on their faces made me think they were unhappy, as well. I was interested in championship matches between big-name wrestlers such as Taiho and Kashiwado as I grew up, but I had never been an eager sumo fan. However, in New York in 1985, the parade of sumo wrestlers represented a race and an ancient culture that greatly contrasted with the modern, Western surroundings. Besides, the tremendous acclamation by the audience roused me. I was beginning to see sumo culture in a new light. The way that it combined martial arts with Shinto, the pantheistic, indigenous religion of Japan, became apparent. Yokozuna Chiyonofuji's elaborate grandchampion ritual even looked like an *ukiyoe* woodblock print from old Japan. The audience cheered loudly as they watched this grand man, steeped in tradition. Of all the Japanese visiting America at that time, the sumo wrestlers were the most warmly welcomed, even more than a prime minister.

The friendly audience, however, started raising clenched fists as they were informed that the tournament would begin. They were ready for the grand sumo tournament, and the hall was thrown into an uproar.

7 *Exercise and Rest*

AS SOON AS the tournament began, the audience had changed from gentlemen to a rowdy crowd. They roared like lions in Africa. They whistled like a hurricane. Had the Americans gotten angry? They sat, started to come out of their seats, stood, applauded, and then sat back down. They repeated these actions each time a new bout started. My seat shook every time. An announcer who seemed to be a real sumo-lover stirred up the spectators' excitement with his quick-witted explanations. The hall was filled with loud voices and constant movement. Do Americans exercise while the players fight? Elderly men looked as excited as the young people; they stood cheering and shaking their fists in mid-air. When the American wrestler, Konishiki, who weighed over 250 kilograms* then, fought with Sakahoko, all the Americans cried out Konishiki's nickname "Sally!" in chorus. The voices of the announcer and the traditionally dressed referee on the *dohyo* were completely drowned out. Someone's drink sprayed onto my neck from behind. Konishiki won the first round and was welcomed with a storm of applause. The air vibrated as if a plane were roaring over my head. How dared the Japanese to have fought against these energetic Americans in the war! I was overcome by the Americans' strong reaction that bore down on me, and I even began to miss the calmer audience at sumo tournaments

---

* 550 pounds.

in Japan. Could the wrestlers perform in such a different atmosphere as this? What I saw through the excited crowd, however, was the happy faces of wrestlers, something that was never seen during the regular tournaments in Japan. When the long struggle on the *dohyo* was over, the audience, which glowed contentedly, gave a very loud cheer for the completely changed wrestlers, who were now disheveled, gasping for breath, and covered with sand. The wrestlers and the audience shared the moment. It was a different, and terrific, way of seeing sumo.

January 12, 1993, two and a half years after my family had returned home to Japan, I went to see a New Year tournament at Kokugikan, Tokyo's sumo arena. On the first floor, in each of the box seats arranged like terraced paddy-fields, I saw elderly people leisurely enjoying sumo as I had expected. Some napped there or ate a box lunch and drank saké, talking loudly with the others in their group. There was the smell of soy sauce all around. Men in costume from a teahouse walked busily through the narrow aisle between the box seats delivering shopping bags stuffed with sumo souvenirs. Women enjoyed talking with each other and frequently burst into raucous laughter. Others wandered up and down and from side to side in the arena. The audience apparently wasn't looking at the center of the pit. This was not during intermission but while the sumo wrestlers were fighting on the *dohyo*. Except for the big matches, the spectators in the box seats seldom got excited. Even during the climax of a bout, they couldn't move freely, partly because they were sitting cross-legged and partly because they had gotten drunk. Of course, they seemed to be happy and relaxed. They looked as if they were relaxing in the living room of their father's house while enjoying sumo.

More than pointing up differences in temperament between Americans and Japanese, the scenes in Madison Square Garden and in Kokugikan brought home to me anew the long history of sumo. The original form of sumo culture, polished through three centuries, has attracted Americans. Tradition in Japan has never hurried people into loving sumo, but it is something that both Americans and Japanese enjoy.

8 *We Lose Our Way*

SATURDAY, June 15, 1985, around 10:30 P.M., my husband was driving our car along the Henry Hudson Parkway in New York on our way back to Fort Lee. Soon we saw the beautifully illuminated George Washington Bridge ahead on the left. Our family was going home after seeing Japan's Grand Sumo Tournament in Madison Square Garden. The excitement of seeing sumo in the brilliantly lighted hall was still vivid in my mind. We would be home in fifteen minutes.

In fifteen minutes, however, we found that we had lost our way. "Where are we?" "That's what I wanted to ask you." "Look at the map!" Our first exciting night in New York had changed into panic. I was sure that we had lost our way before we had taken the road for the George Washington Bridge. I opened to the page with the bridge. We had moved to the United States just two months before. To me, the map's small letters of many unfamiliar street names looked like crawling worms. It puzzled me even more. I looked up and tried to see the names of the streets we were passing at each corner. No signs could be seen in the area. Most of the lights were broken. Few cars passed by, either. Along some of the nearly deserted streets, the headlights of our new '85 white Pontiac 6000 LE lit up smashed cars, dilapidated shop signs, and damaged show windows.

The scenes of urban decay stirred my imagination. Many violent scenes from American movies like "Dirty Harry" came to mind one after the other. In real life, however, Clint Eastwood never came to help. Even the bulky Japanese sumo wrestlers I had seen at Madison Square Garden about thirty minutes earlier were of no help now. Also the sumo tournament's cheers, sweet smell of popcorn, and spotlights immediately vanished into the darkness that was as black as ink. Everything was so still that I could hear my heart beating. I began to worry about whether we would be able to return to our home in Japan alive or not. At that moment, I missed the safe, secure towns in Japan.

After a while, we found a blood-red light streaming out of the slightly open door of a building on the far right corner of the intersection. I had a ray of hope that somebody would tell us the way to the bridge. Our car moved forward slowly, and as we approached the corner, we could see a liquor store sign and a group of people around the door. Some were lying down on the sidewalk holding bottles and others were leaning against the wall. They seemed to be drunk. I almost gave up hope. Our car slowly turned right. When we were about to pass the store, one of those who had been lying down sat up suddenly, stood up, and then began to approach our car. A few men started following him. They all tottered. One lifted his hand. I held my breath.

I urged our older son, a sleepyhead, to check the rear door locks while, with a forced smile, I pretended to be a calm mother. My hands were moist with sweat because of fear. I looked at my husband, who must have been confused too. He said nothing but slightly pinched his nose a few times. I knew he was perplexed. However, he was calm as he slowed down so as not to hit those men. I prayed nothing would happen, but my imagination ran ahead of me; in my mind our family was at the point of death already.

The tottering men came on. Right in front of our car, with open arms, the astonishingly tall men moved like big puppets. The blood-red light of the liquor shop looked like a flame flaring up behind them. Waving bottles in mid-air they all shouted something to us in hoarse voices. I closed my eyes as I felt our car shake.

Even though our car had shaken only because my husband had suddenly put it in reverse, even though the group, perhaps out of kindness, had come to tell us that we had missed the ONE-WAY sign, and even though the sign had been pointing to the ground, it took a while for me to accept the situation. I shivered with fear and at the same time was ashamed of myself for my presumption that the drunken men were going to attack us.

We finally got back to Fort Lee at almost midnight. "We enjoyed the sumo, didn't we?" our younger son, who had been sleeping in the rear seat, said drowsily. I looked up at the modest but heart-warming porch light of our home.

⟨9⟩ *Homework*

OUR TWO sons were promoted, one to the eighth grade, the other to the third grade, in September 1985. After the long summer vacation, they had reverted to feeling like nervous newcomers. Even though they couldn't follow most of their classes yet, they wanted to participate more fully in school life with their American classmates. The older son especially didn't like being a guest any longer. My husband and I had been helping them with their homework from the beginning. We also started to explain what they would be learning the following day in science and social studies. We read the textbooks with them. My husband helped our older son, and I worked with the younger one. Because both brought home a lot of homework, including leftover classwork that they couldn't finish at school, all of our family spent time doing homework in the evening, and sometimes the next morning as well. My husband and I didn't want our younger son to stay up later than nine o'clock, so he went to bed earlier than his brother.

My husband, who had studied at an American graduate school, strictly guided our older son. Even after he had worked long hours at his office in Manhattan, he never missed tutoring our son. Sometimes he sounded stern, but his strong guidance helped his son feel positive about his life in Fort Lee. The older son, fourteen years old then, gradually became more confident in his studies. Though he couldn't speak English yet, he could participate in his class by doing homework and taking tests. When he received the highest score in his class on the science test for the first time, the science teacher, Mrs. Fitzpatrick, praised him generously, and that encouraged him more. He knew he had grasped the American way of learning when he passed the bilingual class and the E.S.L. class.

For me, to help with our younger son's homework certainly was a joy because I liked English. But it kept me busy as well. From the kitchen, frying fish and mincing onions, I loudly answered his questions while he was doing his homework in the dining room next to the kitchen. After dinner, I sat beside him and helped him with his homework. I had majored in English but certainly had never mastered it. Most of the vocabulary in the textbooks was so new to me even though it was for elementary school children. I was a tutor who spent a lot of time consulting the dictionary and couldn't help crying out each time I found an expression I understood in his textbooks. I had never seen everyday words like "scrub" in the old English poems I had learned in my college days. I often wished I could go to school with our younger son and learn English from the very beginning level. A year later, the hours for doing homework became shorter. When one and a half years had passed, he got so that he could notice some mistakes his mother made. One day, about two years after our younger son had transferred to the American public school, he said, "I will do it by myself, Mother." The two years working with him had stimulated my desire to learn English for myself, and I started to write essays in the summer of 1987.

 *A Fine*

WHEN MY friend Kiyoko, the wife of my husband's colleague, found a traffic ticket under the windshield wiper of her car, she turned pale. One afternoon in September 1985, the first year of American life for both of us, she got a ticket at the public parking lot in Fort Lee because her time on the parking meter had expired. That day we had gone to a beauty salon near there while our children went to school. Since I hadn't gotten a driver's license yet, she picked me up and took me to the salon. I, too, was responsible for the ticket. The violation slip said that if she didn't pay by the due date she would have to appear in court as well. "Fine" and "court," which we had had nothing to do with until then, suddenly touched our lives. The scene of poor Kiyoko standing in a court of the United States even flashed into my mind. Later when we looked back on that day, we couldn't help laughing. However, we took it seriously at the time.

Both Kiyoko's and my family had moved from Japan about a half-year earlier. Kiyoko and I were not used to the area yet and were not very fluent in English. Our children also struggled with English in their new schools. Our husbands, who were our last resort, were working hard at the New York branch of a Japanese bank. We all were very busy adapting to basic American life. Besides, knotty problems with my house came up frequently: The basement resident of the duplex let his dog walk in the front yard and never cleaned up after it. Water overflowed from one of our toilets sometimes. Squirrels went in and out of the ceiling through a broken place in the eaves. Moreover, I heard from my mother-in-law that my father-in-law had been injured in a traffic accident in Japan. Kiyoko, too, worried about her daughter's health after she had a high fever. There was a mass of things to make us anxious. Kiyoko's getting the parking ticket was one more mess we had gotten into and which we wanted to solve as soon as possible. With our hair freshly done, Kiyoko and I were at a loss beside her big Buick in the large public parking lot.

I thought that we had better ask someone what we should do. In Japan, police officers generally were people to be trusted. American police officers, however, seemed stern, tough, and willing to fire their guns, like the police in old American TV dramas like "The Untouchables."

They also didn't seem the type to be patient about listening to our poor English. So we waited with resignation for the police car to appear in the public parking lot while trying to think of several English words that might be required. When we saw that the police car was coming, Kiyoko nudged me since I was older than her, and asked me to talk to the police officer.

As I expected, the policeman, who appeared to be in his early fifties, and I, a Japanese woman, couldn't understand each other very easily. It was not because he wasn't patient but because I couldn't speak English well. The honest-looking man strained his ears to catch my words when I explained the situation to him. Then he tilted his head and blinked his eyes. Kiyoko and I held our breath as we waited for his words. Then we alternated between relief and disappointment as he responded. We at least understood that we could pay the fine at the Borough Hall, but we didn't know where it was. We shot imploring glances at the gentleman. "Well . . ." The next moment he started making elaborate gestures as he explained the location. However, the more gestures he made, the farther the Borough Hall seemed to be. An embarrassed atmosphere prevailed among the three of us. At last he seemed to give up as he looked at our frustrated expressions. He promptly got out of the car and opened the door for us. He was so kind that he would take us to the distant destination, I thought. When I made an apology, he said, "It's a piece of cake, ma'am." It was three months later that Kiyoko and I learned the meaning of the idiom "a piece of cake" at the English conversation class in Fort Lee's adult school.

For the first time, we rode in a police car. There was a metal grille on the back of the front seat, probably for protecting police officers from criminals. I could smell something. I regretted my actions a bit because I felt I might have acted hastily at that moment. We two Japanese wives, thirty-two and thirty-nine, sat down on the hard seat meant for criminals, looking at each other awkwardly. He started the car. Kiyoko apologized for troubling him. "No problem, ma'am," he answered through the grille. Kiyoko asked me, "Do you think we will be back in time to pick up the children?" Because I didn't want to ask the police officer such a bothersome question, I answered, "I think so." As we prepared ourselves for the long drive ahead, the car stopped suddenly. "Here we are, ma'am." When the police officer pointed in the direction we had to go, I realized that we had arrived at the Borough Hall. When I heard him say "Take care, and have a nice day, ma'am," I noticed the three of us had only crossed Center Avenue from the public parking lot. It was a ten-second drive. Kiyoko and I entered the building with a blank look on our faces.

"Three dollars!" a clerk at a window of the Parking Authority said bluntly. All the confusion Kiyoko and I had had was just about to go away with three one-dollar bills. We paid half and half, suppressing our laughter in the presence of the clerk, who gave us a suspicious look. When my friend and I left the building, I remembered that the police officer had never fired his gun. Walking to the parking lot, I came to feel as if I would be able to flourish in this host country.

11 *Fallen Leaves*

IN OCTOBER 1985, our family was spending our first autumn in Fort Lee, New Jersey. There were a great many big trees in the town. A lot of leaves fell that season. In the beginning, I raked them as I used to do, remembering our home in Japan.

In 1979 our family owned a house in Japan. It was not a big house with a large garden like those in the United States, however. We planted about twenty trees in our small garden. They were small trees, as tall as a person, but most of them were deciduous. We could make plenty of compost and also enjoy seeing the beautiful fall colors. Yet the houses in Japan, especially in residential areas near Tokyo, stand very close together. What made it worse was that we had high winds in the autumn. The winds blew the leaves everywhere. I had to clean up the garden and street every morning and felt bad when I would see our leaves scattering onto my neighbors' yards. The next-door lady and I used to call out to each other across the fence, "Good morning. Sorry about the leaves." "No, I'm the one who has to apologize. Some of my leaves have blown into your yard."

In Fort Lee, our family lived in a simple duplex that had only one small deciduous tree in the front yard. Almost all of the leaves from our neighbor's yard collected at the front of our garage. Even though I cleaned them up as soon as possible, more leaves came and nobody came to apologize as they would have in Japan. One morning, I was raking leaves as usual and saw a man who lived across the street blowing "his" leaves toward "my" side of the street with his blower. I started to form a sentence in English in my head to stop his bad behavior. When I put the English together, however, a red truck came and sucked up the blown leaves along with my English thoughts. The man across the street closed the door after making sure that there were no leaves around his house. I saw that the mountain of leaves I had raked were left before me. Then, the leaves blew away again. I thought to myself, "When in Rome, do as the Romans do," and at that time quit one of the daily routines I had always done in Japan.

This was the United States, where abundant nature grew on the huge land. Trees grew until they were mature, they spread their arms and legs just like a man stretching himself very comfortably on the spacious land. This was a poetic view of nature and showed a happiness with the earth. Why, I thought, did I have to complain about the fallen leaves? I would rather take delight in trees. I would talk to them in my mind.

Trees,
    shake your branches,
        throw your leaves off as much as you wish.
I will see your high-spirited shape
    in the winter's high sky.
I will hear your tender rustling
    in the spring breeze.
I will rest in your shade
    under the burning summer sun.

Trees,
>   shake your branches,
>   throw your leaves off as much as you wish.
> I will love you as you are.

Was I too generous? Many more leaves have gathered again.

⟨12⟩ *How to Refuse to Be Kissed*

AFTER HE had been promoted to the third grade of School #3 in September of 1985, my younger son took a reading class from his former homeroom teacher Mrs. Benedict because he couldn't follow the new reading class. Though he still couldn't speak English, he was always encouraged in her class. He came to like the teacher much more because sometimes she gave him candy. One day, I heard that she kissed her pupils who gave her presents on the last day of the school year. For a nine-year-old Japanese boy who, ever since he had started to be aware of things around him, hadn't been used to being kissed, this was a serious matter. The rumor was apparently true.

One bright day in May 1986, in the dentist's reception room in Fort Lee, my son and I were waiting our turn. I was reading a book. "That's it!" my son suddenly exclaimed and asked me if I had a piece of paper and a pen. "What happened?" I asked. "Nothing in particular. Hurry, please." He seemed hesitant to explain what he was about to do. I gave him a piece of paper and a pen and he started copying a sign on the wall. The sign said, "Thank you for not smoking." He wrote down "Thank you for not kissing" and looked relieved. "I'll show this to Mrs. Benedict when she starts to kiss me." He put the note into his pants pocket. He must have been worrying about how to refuse a kiss in English. I think he kept it for a while, but I didn't know whether the words worked, as he said no more.

It was seven years later when I found out the truth. August 15, 1993, three years after our family had returned to Japan, we welcomed a close family friend, Elizabeth from Fort Lee, as a guest in our home. Elizabeth, who taught with Mrs. Benedict in School #3, told us about the last day of school that year, and I had an urge to find out about the last day of school in 1986. My son, who was sixteen years old then, confessed at last.

That day in June of 1986, in Mrs. Benedict's classroom, pupils were giving their last-day presents to their teacher. She responded by hugging and kissing them, but one Japanese boy hid his face in his hands when she was going to kiss him, and another boy ran around trying to escape. My son was calm, however, because he was sure that the memo in his pocket would work just as the "Thank you for not smoking" sign did. He presented his gift and with it gave the teacher the piece of paper folded twice. At first she seemed surprised at it, but then read it, beaming at the shy boy. Seeing the teacher's beautiful smile, he felt enormously relieved that she would let him go without a kiss. The teacher was even more pleased by the "Thank you for not kissing" note. She burst into laughter in front of my confused son, then swiftly hugged and kissed him. During the seven years since then, however, the crisis seemed to have changed into a happy memory as well as a reminder of Mrs. Benedict's kindness.

13 *Hannah*

HANNAH PAIGE, my aged neighbor, suddenly went away on a beautiful summer morning in 1988. From my kitchen, twice I heard her shrill voice, "No, I won't go!" Tom, her dog, barked loudly. Then from the window I saw some strange cars—even a police car—and people around her house. In a minute all of them had gone. What had happened? What was the matter with her? Did she do anything wrong? Was it because her husband, William, who had been hospitalized since last fall, hadn't come back home yet or would not come back any longer? I should have asked someone, but I couldn't because I was afraid to find out the truth. Since the last Christmas, I hadn't had a chance to talk to her. We only exchanged greetings. When I rolled up the window shade that morning I saw her taking a walk with Tom as usual. She waved to me as she recognized me from the street. Who would have imagined that she would be taken away suddenly in such a way at that time? Isn't this unusual in the United States? I stood by the window vacantly staring outside. The sky was so clear and seemed to be gazing down into my confusion. A gust of wind shook the trees and it was if the fresh green leaves laughed at me, all at once reflecting the sunshine.

Our family started American life next door to the Paiges in the spring of 1985. Because the Paiges' mail used to be delivered to us by mistake, I would take it over to them. William and Hannah looked like they were in their late eighties. William was friendly from the beginning, but his wife wasn't as open to her new Japanese neighbors. They seemed to have no children and loved Tom as if he were their real child instead. When William was feeling good, he used to work around their house. Wearing overalls, he did things like mow the lawn, make a trellis for cucumbers, and paint the balcony rail, always with Hannah and Tom. They had a small garden in front of the garage. They seeded it in the spring, took care of the growing vegetables in the summer, and harvested them in the fall. They didn't forget to collect the fallen leaves and to make mulch for new soil. They seemed never to dream of entertaining in those days. Hannah never dressed up and always wore inexpensive clothes. She had her own style, however. She sometimes put flowers on her hat and made Tom wear the same color as her dress when they took a walk together. They might have been poor, but they seemed independent. They looked even stately, like soldiers with severe looks rather than the typical sweet elderly people who were generally seen in Japan. They might have been living a life that, for them, was most splendid. I liked seeing them because I could learn many things about life from their routine. Since they had grown old, they spoke loudly. I could hear the sound of their voices every day. It was noisy, but I liked it because I took it as a sign of their being healthy.

For a long time after Hannah had been taken away, the dilapidated blue car, which William used to drive to a nearby supermarket with his wife and Tom, was left parked on the street. Not knowing that the pitiful car had spent good times with its family, the summer sun beamed down on it mercilessly. The grass kept growing. A half-opened window on the second floor rattled sometimes. When I walked by the house, I could imagine hearing Tom's barking and their familiar, loud voices which sounded happy at first and then turned to anguish. I soon realized, however, that I was hearing the August wind rising. Not long after that, some men came and took out the furniture and loaded it onto a truck. They also came to survey the property. I thought the house would be torn down and a new rental house would be built there. Then one morning in the fall, I saw a big dump truck, power shovel, tractor shovel, and a few other vehicles gathered around William and Hannah's house. To me it looked like a party for dinosaurs. They fixed their weird eyes upon the house. "This is the very last chance I have to do anything for Hannah!" I thought as I rushed out of my house with a camera and asked a man who looked like he was in charge if I could take a picture before he started his job. "Sure!" He was generous in giving me space to take pictures. The house stood like a haggard orphan boy whose eyes didn't sparkle even though he saw his favorite dump truck. I said good-bye to the house as I pressed the camera shutter. There was nothing I could do for the Paiges, but I would remember their home for a long time.

In the holiday season of 1985, as a gift to them, I had taken the Paiges a small calendar that had been sent from Japan. William seemed glad to have it, but his wife looked dubious. I realized they might not be Christian; they had no decorations up for Christmas. In 1986, they waited for me. We exchanged greetings and small gifts with each other at the Paiges' front door. That night, I saw a silhouette of a Christmas tree in their window. For me, it looked warmer than other houses and their elaborate illumination. The next morning, I found out that it was just a bare fir branch that William had carelessly cut off a tree in the corner of their front yard. On the morning of December 23, 1987, I found a vinyl bag outside our door when I opened it to see my son off to school. It was a Christmas gift from Hannah: a small jar of homemade pickled cucumbers and a long letter. I knew that William had been hospitalized since the previous fall. A little later, I saw her outside and ran down the steps to thank her. She grasped my hands with her big hands— she was wearing her old gloves that had holes in them—and shot questions at me. "Did you read the letter? Did you taste the pickles? How did you like them?" Her breath scattered in the chill air. When I told her that I liked her pickles very much, she hugged me for the first time, mumbling to herself the way my grandmother had used to do. Then with a pleasant smile she confidently told me that her husband would be back home soon.

The earth shook as the house fell. The dust blew. The

yellow-colored, iron machines assaulted the Paiges' home. They pulled William's trellis down and it broke into pieces. They smashed the window frames. Many glass jars that Hannah had kept in the kitchen were crushed crying for help. All day long I could hear the painful groans of the house being torn down. At sunset, the dust thinned out and vanished. Everything became quiet. That night, through the window I saw that only the concrete walls of the basement were left. They stood silently in the mist. In the pale moonlight, they looked like a small fort where Hannah and William had fought bravely, or a huge tomb that mourned the death of the house. I bit my lip and pressed my forehead against the cold glass. The tears rolled down my cheeks and the glass trembled.

Two long years have turned Hannah's pickles amber color. In my refrigerator, a few pieces still remain in the bottom of the jar. My regret at having avoided confronting her situation settled at the bottom of my heart like dregs in the stagnant vinegar. She might have been limited financially, with too many difficulties for her to bear alone, and finally had to be taken away under the law of the United States. However, so far as I had seen, she had her own outlook on life and tried to continue her life at home as long as she could. Her independent way of life even contrasted with the modest one of many aged Japanese people who lived with their son or daughter in Japan. It also showed me that there are many limitations that people still needed to overcome in this free nation, too. She was a very American lady, and she was my friend.

14 *Fairness*

"FAIR" MIGHT be the word that I heard most frequently while I lived in the United States. My children learned that they must behave in a fair manner at school every day. The media carried pictures of angry Congressmen with clutched fists yelling, "Japan should be fair!" from Capitol Hill. Even in a checkout line at the supermarket, everyone would blame somebody who tried to cut in front of others! That the people had the courage to express their convictions was admirable. Americans' belief in being fair seemed to be firm at any time and in any place.

However, I knew there were also exceptions. In the post office at Fort Lee, New Jersey, there was a middle-aged, earnest, and handsome-looking postal clerk. He seldom smiled but always was fair to the customers. He used to tell even a person who looked like he was in a hurry to stand in line, as he added firmly, "You're not the only one in a hurry. Everybody's waiting their turn." People in the line seemed satisfied. One warm day in May 1989, however, a glamorous woman rushed into the post office and went directly to the window of the clerk as he was saying, "Next, please."

There were about six customers then. I happened to be taking my place at the end of the line. The woman, who had a mass of curly hair, was excessively perfumed and wore a tight, low-cut, leopard-print dress. One by one, a few old ladies in the line looked at her and gasped, "Oh, my God!" but said nothing more. The rest of the customers, old gentlemen, too, might have forgotten to blame the unfair woman at that time. Their attention was completely focused on her hips slowly swinging from side to side. Even the handsome window clerk didn't warn her. He blushed a little and, in fact, looked happy to be answering her. After she left, everybody stared at the clerk. The uncomfortable atmosphere of the place made him do his job in an exceedingly modest manner for a while.

The world around us is filled with unfair things. Even though this is a world in which honesty doesn't often pay, we shouldn't permit unfair behavior. The reason why a dishonest act doesn't seem to be forgivable, especially to Americans, might be because their ancestors or they themselves had come to the country with the extraordinary expectation that all classes of people should be treated equally. Every time I heard the word, I was sensitive to the determination that Americans must have had to uphold the excellent virtue of fairness.

15 JFK

THE FIRST picture to be televised via satellite from the United States to Japan was on the morning of November 23rd, 1963 (Japan time). It was the news clip of the assassination of the United States' thirty-fifth President, John Fitzgerald Kennedy. To Japan, which had long wanted to have a broadcast relay with the United States, this first-day linkup turned out to be much more than we had expected, due to the tragedy. The President was a young, celebrated American hero, whom many Japanese adored at the time. He seemed different from other Presidents of the United States; he held a special place in many people's hearts. His attractive speeches, presence in public, and photographs with his family in newspapers fascinated my mother and older sisters. A high school student then, I didn't know why he was killed. A big bright star seemed to have disappeared from the world. The scene of his assassination in Dallas, Texas, at 12:30 P.M., November 22, 1963, was stamped on my memory.

In 1974, our family lived in Philadelphia because my husband was a graduate student at the Wharton School. Our first son was three then. At the end of the summer we visited President Kennedy's birthplace, at 83 Beals Street, Brookline, Massachusetts. It was five years after the house had become a national historic site. Many tourists of all generations came on sightseeing buses. The house had three stories and was painted blue with white window frames. It looked small for a standard American house but was clean and noble. The Stars and Stripes made the house look grand. A tall guard wearing a blue uniform with a shoulder strap stood on the porch and gave the place a dignified atmosphere. Before they entered, tourists mostly looked at the front of the house at first and then up at the roof, as if they expected to see a cross at the top of a church spire. The glorious air that filled the inside of the house seemed to overwhelm all the tourists.

Another Kennedy tragedy, the assassination of the President's brother Robert in 1968, may have made the house seem more sacred. In front of each room some of the visitors stood straight, as if they still felt a sense of loyalty to the President, and some had tears in their eyes, feeling sad about the life of the great young President. I knew that he had been the leader of the United States as well as a beloved son of the United States. I was sure the image of the President I had had in Japan was close to the one that the Americans had, too. At that time I was more interested in the reactions of the people than the interior decoration of the house, which was hard to see because of the crowd. I felt close to the American tourists sharing each moment with them in the house. The taped, confident voice of the President's mother resounded in each room. As I stood among these tall people I listened to her voice as if it were a lecture on how to make a happy home.

After returning to Japan for about ten years, my husband was assigned to the New York branch of a Japanese bank. We resumed our American life in Fort Lee, New Jersey, in 1985, and on April 4, 1988, we visited the Kennedy house again. It was a rainy Monday. This time we took our younger son, who had been born in 1976. My husband drove there because the sightseeing bus didn't take the same route as in 1974. Twenty-five years had already passed since President Kennedy had been assassinated in 1963. It had stopped raining by the time we arrived. It was spring. Beals Street was silent. The wet trunks of the bare trees stood in a milky fog. Only a few cars were parked far apart on the right side of the slightly curving street. When I saw that the color of the house had been changed to green, I was disappointed because it had lost its stately appearance. We didn't see a guard on the porch. The front door was closed and there was a sign that said the entrance was in the back. We went to the back and rang the doorbell as if we were visiting our neighbor. A young female guide welcomed us and showed us to the basement, where we waited for about fifteen minutes until the other visitors came down. The taped voice of Mrs. Rose Kennedy echoed throughout the house as it had in 1974. Another guide, a middle-aged man, took two elderly ladies downstairs as they finished touring inside. The tourists silently went out of the house and we were the only tourists left there. Then the young guide took us upstairs.

We started the tour in the living room. There was the piano that I had remembered. Then in the dining room we saw the dining table and a small table with a couple of chairs by the window, which was for little children who couldn't behave with good table manners. The huge black stove in the kitchen, the President's christening dress which had turned almost gray with age in the nursery room on the second floor, the pictures on the wall in the narrow hall, the index cards recording the Kennedy children's health conditions on the small desk in the sewing room— all these were where they had been before, but they had faded considerably. The taped voice of Mrs. Rose Fitzgerald Kennedy, who was ninety-eight years old at the time of our visit, sounded unnaturally vivacious in the empty house. It was as if a mother who had lost her sons were making a speech forcing herself to appear strong, and the voice evoked sympathy rather than admiration. I listened to it as if it were a lecture on life. Trying to survive seemed to mean that we often had to admit that we were mortal. The house might have been dedicated to the mother of the President, not to the nation, after all. Years have passed and the world has been changing all along.

Questions about President Kennedy's assassination and character remain unresolved in the minds of many people. Nevertheless, as far as I have seen, in the United States the Kennedy name has seemed to hold onto a certain status as time has passed and sometimes it even evokes the impression of a royal family. They said that the President's fame might have been made by the wealth and ambition of his father, Joseph P. Kennedy, not by his political ability; or that the President created his fame by the media-enhanced image of himself. What I would say is that the man who appeared in front of cameras was always himself until the very last moment of his life. In my mind, the President is still a symbol of a graceful America of that time, and serves as a reminder of my adolescence and Japan's growth in the 1960s.

16 *To Dye or Not to Dye*

"WHY DOESN'T Barbara Bush get her hair dyed? She looks like the *mother* of the new President!" One afternoon in the fall of 1988, a middle-aged woman called in to a radio program to state her opinion of the new First Lady of the United States. How frankly the woman talked about such personal matters! I was surprised to hear it at first, but then realized that it was not only the woman on the radio but also other people who recommended that the new First Lady should dye her hair. It might have been because many American people felt a new closeness with Mrs. Bush. As I thought about it, however, I came to realize that coloring one's hair seemed to be so normal for American people.

While I lived in Fort Lee, New Jersey, across the Hudson River from New York City, in the second half of the 1980s, I used to see many blondes everywhere I went. Especially in New York, businesswomen with blond hair looked dashing and sexy. They had a proud look as if they were the freest women in the whole world. They confidently walked the streets, their bright hair waving in the wind. Their hair color surely matched the image of Manhattan. I used to think that not only the skyscrapers but blondes seemed to embody American's lust for wealth, power, and freedom. Most of those women, however, were artificial blondes. Their original hair color was obviously not blond. I could see their dark roots. In the beginning, I ridiculously assumed that the color of their hair turned blond as their hair got longer, because there were so many blondes. I soon came to know the truth, but it wasn't as easy to understand why they wanted to become blondes. The purpose couldn't only be so-called rejuvenation. They were in the prime of life. They looked independent, and I thought they would be beautiful even if they were not blond. Not all American gentlemen seemed to prefer blondes as the title of the old film says. It might have been something like a status symbol among some white people in the United States. If anything, in fact, I didn't like women who turned into fake blondes. They were put on a pedestal in commercials, yet they seemed to hold themselves in contempt by pretending to be more beautiful than they really were.

New York was filled with an exalted air in every corner of the streets. People, both good- and ill-natured, seemed absorbed in looking for chances to make money. In the city, they had a lot of self-confidence and always asserted themselves. Gradually, I came to think that dyeing their hair blond might have been one of the ways women survived in New York. They also seemed to be fighting against the male chauvinism of the nation. When women got angry with men as they insisted on their rights, their long blond hair seemed to be about to wave like a lion's mane or their short blond hair seemed to be about to stand on end like a cat's. At the same time, however, such tough blondes could also act weak and coquettish according to time and circumstance. At night, in theaters and restaurants, they apparently liked men to caress their soft-as-down hair. Being blond seemed quite convenient. Everybody likes to be beautiful. I myself put on make-up and will color my hair dark when it turns gray. The blondes' straightforward way of living and their cheerful smiles won me over, as I was liberated from my way of thinking. Choosing a way of life depended on a woman's individual sense of values and aesthetic feeling. I got so that I took women dyeing their hair blond as a matter of course in Western countries. My view at the time was based on what I had seen in the United States.

At the end of July 1990, our family spent two days in London on the way back to Japan after our five-year stay in the United States. When we took the subway trains and saw many commuters on the second evening, I knew that attitudes about women's hair color had not always been the same in Western countries. The British women hadn't dyed their hair. Their genuinely dark hair color seemed to modestly enhance London's grand, elaborate structures built in the eighteenth and nineteenth centuries. The women's appearance was so quiet, and the self-possessed expressions on their faces made me wonder if the traditions of England might have brought some pressure to bear upon them.

We got off the train near our hotel and walked along the hard, worn-away stone pavement. I thought of the America we had left a day ago. It was a country whose people had chosen to become Americans. They must have been ready to make something different of themselves from the beginning of their American life. They also may have been apt to change their hair color much more readily than I had expected. It was twilight. The big moon rose in the sky with a purple tint. My black hair was swinging in the wind.

17 *The Language Problem*

LIVING ABROAD with a family, generally speaking, is a wonderful experience. In the beginning, however, there are many problems to be overcome to fit into the new environment. One of them is the language problem.

In April 1985, our family started a new life in Fort Lee, New Jersey, and our two sons were faced with this problem at their schools. In Fort Lee there were many foreign children whose fathers had transferred to companies in the New York metropolitan area. The language problem seemed to be serious for many of them.

"When can I go to the bathroom? When can I get a drink of water? How can I say it in English? What are my American classmates talking about now? Why are they laughing? What do the letters mean on the blackboard?" For the new pupils who transferred from abroad, to be in a place where an unknown language was spoken seemed to be much harder than expected. They sat at their desks for six hours a day whether they liked it or not. Not all of them were from Japan. However, due to Japan's expanding overseas business, many of them were Japanese children. In the 1985–86 school year when my sons transferred to the public schools, Fort Lee had 407 Japanese pupils out a total enrollment of 2,476 students from kindergarten to twelfth grade.* Some of them were newcomers.

* From a table of "Japanese/Korean Enrollment, Five-Year Comparison." Fort Lee School District, Fort Lee, New Jersey, 1990.

It was easy to imagine that most American homeroom teachers might have had mixed feelings toward the many pupils who weren't able to respond to the teachers' questions immediately. Our younger son's class usually had four Japanese children in a class of twenty every year. In Japan, however, few foreign families had lived outside of Tokyo before our family left there in 1985. If Japan's public schools had as many foreign pupils as the American schools did, it would throw the Japanese homeroom teachers into a flurry. So far as I saw in the American schools our sons went to, however, no teacher showed any sign of confusion, no classmate looked at the foreign children with curious eyes, and no school staff members discriminated against the shy children. I came to understand that this was because of the Fort Lee Board of Education's practical overall program for welcoming children from other countries. The E.S.L. class and the bilingual class were provided to help students fit into the American schools by teaching them English step by step. Until our sons passed the classes, the teachers eased their difficulties and always seemed to make an effort to fill the cultural gap between the United States and other countries. As a foreign mother, I couldn't thank them enough for their thoughtfulness.

Until the language problem of the foreign children could be solved, many of their families must have struggled. I, too, was always anxious about our two sons and the stress they felt in their schools, so from the bottom of my heart I hoped and waited for the day they would be able to understand English. I am not a Christian, but what came readily to my mind then was a phrase from the Bible, "In the beginning was the Word."* For our family, The Day came first to our younger son, a fourth-grader then. One evening after he had spent a year and a half in School #3, he was hanging around me in the kitchen and suddenly loudly said, "I wondered why I was feeling happy all day today and I realized the reason now. Mother, I could understand everything that was said in English at school!" A few months later, our older son, a high school student then, said coolly, "It took a long time." Then they were finished with the E.S.L. and bilingual classes and could join the regular curriculum.

Since our sons had become familiar with English, they began to relax. In their schools they sometimes helped newcomers from Japan as they had been helped in the beginning. They also invited American friends to our home. They enjoyed summer camps and acquired the habit of listening to American music. Our older son started to watch MTV before supper and bought records by Bon Jovi and Don Johnson. Our younger son enjoyed attending his classmates' many birthday parties which were held at their homes, a roller-skating rink, or movie theaters. He also had great fun having water-fights with his classmates. Both sons once attended the opening ceremony for Fort Lee's Constitution Park wearing the same "Just Say NO" T-shirt as all the other schoolchildren.

Around the time when our family had spent four years in the United States, I noticed that our sons came to insist on their own opinions. To express themselves, they used

* John 1:1.

gestures that American boys used, as well. In 1989, the fifth summer of our sojourn in Fort Lee, our younger son, who was enjoying summer camp, said, "Mother, if our family stays in the United States forever, it will be all right with me." They seemed to have forgotten that they had struggled with English in the beginning.

In 1990, when we returned home to Japan, I saw the Stars and Stripes on the wall over the desk of our older son who had gotten back home a year earlier. I was keenly aware that our sons had been a part of American society and learned more than the English language in the United States.

Our family resumed our lives in Japan after five years and four months of American life. I think of the phrase from the Bible, "In the beginning was the Word" again. Our younger son now is faced with a new problem: the Japanese language.

⟨18⟩ *Determination*

"CAN I work at the doll-making class? That's out of the question. I have neither a license nor teaching experience. I haven't driven my car along Route 4 yet. I'm not good at speaking and understanding English, as you well know." That was my immediate response when my friend Kimiko asked me if I would like to teach the doll-making class organized by the Senior Services Center at the Town House near Route 4 in Teaneck, New Jersey. Every Wednesday morning, from 10:15 to 12:00, a doll-making class for senior citizens was held there, and a few Japanese women volunteered to teach the class. Kimiko was a volunteer instructor and needed help because one instructor had quit. My head filled with negative ideas. However, Kimiko's smile and encouragement brought me there on Wednesday, October 7, 1987, to observe the class. It was just eight minutes from my house. The Town House was a brick building located on the corner of Forest Avenue and Teaneck Road, next to a school.

Certainly, I wanted to become familiar with as many Americans as possible while I lived in the United States. However, I had never imagined that I would spend time with old ladies, of all people. Old women in general looked rather gloomy and were full of complaints about their surroundings. When I entered the classroom, however, I realized I had been wrong. It was still ten minutes before 10 o'clock, but six ladies were already working on their dolls and chatting happily. Though you couldn't say they were young, they looked much more pleasant, charming, and relaxed than I had expected. They seemed to be sociable and independent. I sensed affection in their expressions when they welcomed me. Another instructor, Eriko, was already at work. Since Kimiko and Eriko were taking college courses on Wednesday afternoon, they had to leave the class a little early. I watched how Eriko and Kimiko were instructing the ladies and wondered whether I could do it or not. I helped the instructors with small jobs. I heard from Kimiko that Eriko had been volunteering at the doll-making class for over two years, and Kimiko had joined her last spring. The class seemed to depend on Eriko and love Kimiko. Referring to their dolls, they asked, "Eriko, could you put hair on my daughter's head?" or "Kimiko, would you cut the fabric for a new doll body?" The instructors also explained how to stitch the pieces of the fabric together. They looked busy. As I was admiring the skill of the two instructors, Eriko approached me holding a piece of bias tape, a tiny collar, and a bodice of the small dress for some lady's doll, and whispered, but in Japanese so as not to be heard by the class, "Mrs. Koyano, I am confused about how I should put this collar on this dress." This unexpected request for help pleased me. I showed her how to put the collar and the bias tape on the bodice. Eriko whispered, "Thank you. Although I'm sometimes unsure of myself, I love this class. I'm happy I have the time to volunteer." Later, I wondered if Eriko had been discreetly trying to help me relax, because up to that time she was doing everything very well. Then Eriko left to go to her college classes. About thirty minutes later, around 11:00, Kimiko also had classes to attend, so I left with her. Even though I wasn't responsible for them yet, I felt a little sorry for the ladies because they had to continue for one more hour without an instructor.

I spent the rest of the day thinking about the class. The atmosphere of the class was comfortable, and both Eriko and Kimiko were kind. I liked sewing. In my childhood, I remembered, I used to make many dresses for my dolls while sitting next to my mother, who had been very good at sewing. Two and a half years had already passed since our family moved to the United States. I had been busy helping our sons adjust to school life and they had come to understand much more English than I had. My husband seemed to be confident about his assignment in New York, as well. I should try something new, I thought. Now might be the time for me to start enjoying my American life. I may not be an instructor like Kimiko and Eriko, but at least I'll be able to be a good helper. Even though I can't speak English well, I'll be able to make myself understood to the ladies using gestures. Since I've been driving for two years, I'll be able to drive along Route 4, too. I'll call Kimiko tomorrow morning. I had made up my mind.

19 *The Needle with the Red Thread*

SOON AFTER I started volunteering at the senior citizens' center in October 1987, a feeble-looking old woman, who seemed to be in her early nineties, was brought to the class by Camille, the director of the center. The woman, whose name was Mrs. Duncan, wouldn't speak to anyone in the class and didn't seem to be interested in making dolls. Camille must have been at a loss about what to do with her.

On the first day, she just sat in class and remained withdrawn. During her second class, a woman named Florence invited her to sit next to her and asked me to cut a doll pattern for the silent member. When I cut the fabric for her, she took it but didn't say anything. Florence looked at me as if to apologize for her. Mrs. Duncan looked a bit fragile, and I was afraid she couldn't hold a needle with her thin fingers. But she started stitching as if the needle awakened her. Her hands trembled and her arms moved slowly like a machine that needed oiling, but she gave me the impression that she had sewn many dresses in the prime of her life. I felt sorry to have chosen such a simple pattern for that lady. I sat beside her and sometimes talked to her about the stitching. She didn't respond at all. Eriko and Kimiko were busy helping other ladies. Florence sometimes talked to her in a warm, friendly way, but I was not yet used to communicating with withdrawn, elderly ladies like her.

I pinned; she stitched. We kept silent in the room that was filled with cheerful conversations. Mrs. Duncan concentrated on sewing as if she were eagerly talking to the red-colored clothes about her long life. The needle might have been her only friend who could convey her thoughts faithfully. It wasn't just her; the rest of the class was also quiet while they stitched. I remembered my family in Japan: my grandmother, who had died long ago, my mother, and my mother-in-law all used to sew silently, thinking about something. The long, thin piece of polished steel, in a sense, absorbed their thoughts through their fingertips. Gradually, however, I thought that I would try to reach out to Mrs. Duncan even if she wouldn't react to me.

I put the pins closer together, giving her fewer stitches

to finish with her slow hands. She looked a bit dubious at first but finished stitching earlier than before and waited for me to come back from helping the other women. She also began to look at me frequently though she didn't smile back. I enjoyed imagining what she was thinking of me. Although there wasn't any conversation between us for a few weeks, we looked at each other, touched fingers, and seemed to trust each other. Sometime before Thanksgiving Day, the stitching was almost finished. When I said to her, "We can do the stuffing next week, can't we?" unexpectedly she relaxed the expression on her face at last and said, "Thank you." It was weak but was the very voice I had been waiting for. Moreover, she smiled stiffly. She may have put forth her greatest effort in doing so. Her real voice and the sweet expression on her face were more than I deserved. I was at a loss for a reply and only held her cold hands in mine. For the first time she left the materials for the stuffed doll in my charge. This modest reciprocal flow of feeling between us helped me settle down to my volunteer job as a doll-making teacher.

Mrs. Duncan never came back. In the summer of 1990, when I quit the class to leave the United States, I saw that the needle with red-colored thread which she had stuck in the fabric about three years before was still shining, not rusted. It reminded me of the spark she had shown when she sewed beside me.

20 *Instructors*

TWO YEARS had passed since I had taken over the volunteer job from the former instructors, Eriko, who had moved to Detroit, and Kimiko, who had left for Japan. As Kimiko had recommended that I do this volunteer work earlier, I invited Takako, my neighbor, to the class. Eriko left the job in the care of her friend Yoshimi. When Yoshimi quit, her young friend Yoko replaced her. So I had been working with Takako and Yoko for the past two years. We were the wives of men who worked for Japanese companies in the New York metropolitan area. Consequently, we had to say good-bye to the class when our husbands' assignments in New York were over. I heard that a Japanese wife who loved dolls had started the class long ago, maybe fifteen years earlier. Japanese wives generally didn't have a work visa in the United States, and the sphere of our action was limited. The class was one of the few places where we could take part in American society.

Our job was to teach and help ladies make dolls. There weren't any sewing machines in the room; we made it a rule to sew by hand. All the members of the class decided which doll they wanted to make from pictures in textbooks. They were Americans, people of individuality; they would never all make the same doll together. I loved such an independent way of choosing. At the same time, however, it required the three of us to do many things. For each doll, we chose the material from our stock in the storage closet when the student didn't have any. We also made patterns, cut fabrics, pinned them together, and explained briefly how to stitch them. When they had finished the parts of the body, we gave them stuffing and explained how to put the parts together. We cut yarn for the hair and put it on the doll's head. Then we cut fabrics for the underwear, dress, apron, and shoes. We explained how to sew them, and sometimes drew on the faces. On average, there were ten students in attendance. We were busy but we managed to enjoy coffee and brief conversations with the students each week. We had birthday parties for everyone, too.

In the class we made many kinds of dolls: a baby, a grandma, a boy, a girl, a pussycat, a puppy, a teddy bear, a clown, Adam and Eve, a Japanese doll, and so on. The baby doll, girl doll (large or small), puppy doll, and the Japanese girl doll were always popular among the ladies. Everyone in the class loved their dolls like their own babies. They hoped their dolls would be well made, and the room filled with shouts of joy and envy each time someone completed one. However, the members' own ideas about the dolls sometimes didn't work: The width of someone's teddy bear doubled when she finished stuffing it, because her favorite fabric stretched. A puppy doll couldn't stand up since its stomach had been packed too full as the student had lost herself in talk; it needed an operation. A girl doll that had been expected to be innocent-looking turned out sexy because of the bright-colored dress.

The class not only had dolls but also some regular visitors. Because there was a big scale near the door inside the room, gentlemen who attended a wood-carving class in the senior citizens center would often loom into the class to check their weight and were usually teased by somebody about joining the doll-making class. A quiet lady, Betty, who was from Germany, would come into the classroom to water a potted plant. An instructor of a craft class, Louise, would come in to take some materials for her class from the storage closet and enjoyed talking with us for a while. A long-time member of the class, Alice, always came to kiss everybody. Mary, who was very beautiful, used to come to show herself off in her color-coordinated outfits. A lady who had been to Japan came to talk about it with us. "The subway trains in Tokyo were so clean!" she said with surprise. The class had a very comfortable atmosphere. Neither the silent dolls nor the pleasant people ever gave me a dull moment.

My colleagues, Takako, five years younger than I, and Yoko, a half-generation younger than I, were bright women. Takako always made a point of smoothing the wrinkled fabric with an iron before cutting it, so that it would be pretty. She had a good sense for matching colors and helped the ladies when they were confused, because the choice of the color of the cloth influenced the results. She also helped a student get a girl doll ready in time for her granddaughter's birthday; Takako took the doll home and finished it. Later, the lady eagerly told us how crazy her granddaughter was about the birthday gift. The youngest instructor, Yoko, was calm and earnest. She sometimes even practiced making dolls at home. When we made the Japanese doll, Yoko tried and succeeded in making the complicated head of the doll. This was a big improvement for us all. Everybody asked her to make the doll heads from then on. The three of us were rather quiet instructors. In my case, it was because I couldn't speak English fluently. But this was the country in which the right to speak freely was guaranteed; the ladies in the class never kept it to themselves when they thought something was strange. They got angry with us if they thought that they were treated unfairly or if they had to wait a long time for their turn. Gradually, these strong American ladies made us speak up more. The more explanation they received, the more deeply they came to trust us. In the fall of 1988 and 1989, Takako, Yoko, and I were honored before all the members of the center. We were very glad to be appreciated by them.

In class, I really was called one of the "instructors" because I could read the printed instructions more quickly, use scissors and needles more easily, and move to find materials in the storage closet more swiftly than the students could. This was just because I was younger than they were. When I was small, I used to play with dolls. I was the youngest in the family. I commanded and loved my dolls as my family had taken care of me. I had enjoyed designing all the dresses for my dolls, too. So this was a natural as well as an enjoyable job for me to be doing. My involvement with many American ladies who loved dolls enriched my life. They taught me that we had many things to share with each other, even though we came from different cultures. They taught me that we can enjoy ourselves even when we get old. They were my instructors in life.

21 *Different Customs*

IN A SENSE, the doll-making class was a place where two cultures clashed. Especially when we expressed our feelings, the differences between Americans and Japanese were visible. American ladies in the class used to hug and kiss occasionally, but we Japanese instructors didn't express our feelings in such demonstrative, physical ways.

One of the members of the class, Alice, who was in her late eighties then, didn't make dolls any longer but came to the class only to kiss everybody and say, "God bless you!" When I had first come to the class, I remembered, I was surprised and confused to see that she was coming to hug me with open arms. I unintentionally stepped backward and then kept standing against the sink in the corner of the room just rolling my eyes up and down as she kissed me. The class noticed it. Such reactions, however, were repeated more or less every time a new Japanese volunteer took part in the class. Bowing one's head to another woman when first meeting, as Japanese would naturally do, didn't seem to serve any purpose as a form of greeting in the class.

There were other ladies in the class who liked to hug and kiss. Once I was almost smothered by Martha's breasts because she hugged me tightly, holding her completed doll in her hand. A vivacious lady, Hazel, embarrassed me: with an exaggerated swinging of her hips she used to approach me as she pursed her lips. A kind lady, Rose, made a point of hugging me in a motherly way when she wanted to show her feelings. All the ladies kissed me on both cheeks on my birthday. Their way of showing affection was different from mine, but I liked it. At the same time, however, the more demonstrative the American ladies were, the lonelier they seemed to be somehow. I could give them neither a hug nor a kiss, myself, because I hadn't become familiar with behaving in such an American way. But in addition to talking to them, I remembered the ladies' first names, smiled at them, and gave their dolls loving hugs. These actions might have been too simple but were natural for me as a way to show my friendliness toward the members of the class.

In three years I got so that I was able to respond in class. When the women hugged me, I tried to put my arms around them but usually couldn't because they were too big. When I explained to some lady how to stitch, I would put my hand on her back or shoulder. It was helpful for me to convey my feelings to the ladies that way because I couldn't express them well enough in English. When I was busy cutting cloth for a doll's dress, I boldly put out my cheek to make Alice's kissing easier and I enjoyed her reaction: "Oh, you're ready!" In my childhood, I remembered, my parents used to hug me. I too kissed my sons on the forehead as I said good night to them when they were small. Even though it was not common to hug and kiss in Japan as a form of greeting in public, it didn't seem in the least to affect the way I behaved in the class. I came to think I would be able to hug someone whenever she needed it.

One day, however, I found I couldn't. When I heard that Rose had lost her brother a few days previously, I never even imagined that I would try such public display. "Rose, are you all right?" I repeated. I just sat close beside her. She had tears in her eyes. I felt her trembling next to me as I sewed a tiny doll dress for her. In this situation, I unconsciously behaved as I had used to do in Japan, after all. What I felt sure about then was that she was important to me.

22 *Ladies I Love*

FOR THE first two years I volunteered, I met many ladies who loved dolls, and I came to know the roles of each member of the class. I will introduce each of them briefly here.

Elmie was wonderful. She always sat near the classroom door. She liked to make dolls very much, and she also liked to go to Atlantic City, New Jersey, to gamble. When she won, she talked about it a lot in class. Elmie frequently served us coffee and showed us beautiful pictures of her grandchildren. I was happy to help when she asked me to apply her eye lotion after she had an eye operation.

Edith Dunson liked reading books as much as making dolls. I often saw her reading while she was waiting her turn. That was why she preferred making dolls that appeared in stories. Once she made Adam and Eve dolls.

They were the Adam and Eve who hadn't yet eaten the forbidden fruit, so they were naked. It embarrassed me when I explained to Edith how to stitch Adam's private parts together, because I didn't know the words in English. I assumed that the words I knew for the parts of the body were in German, because I had studied German in my college days. Although I was embarrassed, I asked Edith how Americans said it. She looked at me suspiciously, then answered quickly and added, "You should know that already since you're married!" The members of the class giggled. The subject seemed to have taken an unexpected course. If I had been Edith, I would have answered quietly and modestly so as not to embarrass the other person. At first I couldn't catch what she said, but Elmie, sitting next to Edith, saw that I was confused. She was so kind that she stood up and repeated the word twice, loudly and clearly. The classroom burst into laughter and I blushed. In my ignorance I hadn't realized that the word was the same in English as it was in German. It was funny.

Doris would just sit quietly and sometimes doze comfortably by the window. I heard that she used to make dolls before her eyes became bad. She was fashion-conscious and wore a red hat sometimes. Louise, an instructor of another craft class in the center, always came into the doll class, saying, "Doris, are you behaving yourself?" When Doris felt well, she washed the knives and forks after our monthly birthday parties, or she took the attendance sheet back to the office. I was glad to see that she sat in the class.

Ola had become a member of the class recently and

made a wonderful big doll as her first project. It was so pretty. I missed her doll after it was finished. She liked quilting too. She seemed to be very interesting, and I enjoyed getting to know her better.

Ann was a friendly lady. Because she had been sick, she couldn't finish her Japanese doll for a while. She was from Armenia and had been a professional dressmaker.

Audrey took a long vacation in Vancouver, Canada, at the home of one of her many children. When she was in the class, she helped us instructors as a nice interpreter. Did she understand Japanese? No, she didn't. But she understood what we wanted to explain, especially to new members who were not familiar with our English. She had many children, maybe ten—"because," she said one day, "television had not been invented yet when my husband and I were young. We were free at night." All the class laughed at that.

Cynthia joined the class late. She started making a Japanese doll as her first project. She was an earnest and polite lady.

Rose's presence was important to the class. Her seat was always against the window, facing Elmie, and nearest to my place. She sat there working quietly on her doll. Sometimes she taught me English words and wondered why Japanese people didn't speak English well even though they wrote it beautifully. She teased me and even spoiled me. One day, when she asked me how my mother was, I answered, "I hope she's fine," because I hadn't written to her for a while. Around 12 o'clock, before Rose left the class, she came up to me and whispered, holding my shoulders from behind, "Yuko, will you do me a favor?" I wondered what she wanted. Then she said, "Please write to your mother. She must be worrying about you." Though I was ashamed of being advised to do what I should have done in the first place, I promised to write to my mother. Rose's words and actions were effective enough to remind me of my mother. I wrote a heartfelt letter to my mother, the first I had written to her in a long time. The next week, before I mailed it, I brought the sealed letter to class and showed it to Rose. After looking at it, she stood up, hugged me tightly, and said, "Oh, you are a good girl, I am proud of you." To my great regret, I didn't have any idea what I should say at such an unexpected sweet moment. Rose, I was happy to be spoiled by you!

Rita was a quiet, gentle lady. She always sat next to Rose, and she made pretty dolls one after another. I loved them. One of them was a lovely clown. She liked to listen when Yoko, Takako, and I talked about traditional customs in Japan.

Edith Shepherd was a faithful lady. Whenever she talked about people in trouble in the world, tears easily came to her eyes. In speaking to me so directly, she often led me to speak my mind in English. Because she had learned Spanish, she taught us three how to count in Spanish. I remembered only *uno*. We taught her the word for "cute" in Japanese, *kawaii*. She couldn't remember it by the next week.

Louise, a relative of Edith Shepherd, had been a member of a former doll-making class and had come back to the class recently. She seemed to like straw hats. In the beginning, she often used the former instructor's name, Atsuko, for my name, Yuko. Not only Atsuko but also other former instructors were still remembered by some members in the class. I think Louise must have enjoyed her previous class, too. With us, she made a pretty standing doll.

Ethel was quiet and eager. As she sat near Elmie, she pleasantly went about making many beautiful dolls. She had a daughter who was my age. I thought she must be a happy wife because once I saw her husband when he came to pick her up from class, and he looked nice.

Mary Louise was a new member of the class. She was a gentle person, and when she talked to us she whispered. She said that was because she couldn't speak English fluently. "Me, too!" I said to her. Therefore, we three teachers and Mary Louise whispered with one another. She made a standing doll.

Martha was nice. When she was in the class, the atmosphere of the room became more cheerful. She was the first lady who gave me the confidence to do the job, because in the fall of 1987, Martha wanted to make a Japanese geisha-girl doll using the body of regular girl doll with a big round face, fat stomach, and short legs. I helped her for four weeks as my first big job. Though it might not have been a slender doll, she was delighted to see the completed doll and named it after me.

Alice had been a perpetual member of the class for fifteen years. Since she was charming and funny, everybody loved her. She usually came to hug and kiss everybody in the class, saying, "God bless you!" She was the lady who made me get used to being hugged and kissed. When she didn't come into the class, I missed her. One day, I said to myself as I looked at the door of the classroom, "Alice hasn't come in yet today, has she?" Rose heard that and teased me, saying, "You must miss kissed, Yuko."

Muriel was a lively, beautiful person. She looked young for her age. When she was very happy, I felt as if I caught some of her happiness. She was also creative, making a new type of baby doll with a ready-made rubber face and hands, with one hand holding a bottle.

Betty was ninety years old, I think. She made a pretty doll for her three-month-old great-great-granddaughter. Betty stitched the doll and dress quickly and finished them neatly. One morning, a few weeks later, she was sitting in the class when I entered the room. As she recognized me, she stood up, tottering a little and said, "I can't make dolls anymore, but I came here to see you." Walking slowly with her cane, she left the class. I instinctively bowed my head to that respected lady who had given me a moment of honor.

Dora hadn't returned to the class since she had gone home holding her big doll in a shiny red dress. Hilija, who had gone home with a baby doll, and another lady who liked kewpie dolls hadn't come back either, and I missed them.

 *Hospitality*

ON DECEMBER 6, 1989, the doll-making class welcomed a new lady who looked to be in her late eighties. She didn't seem to want to join the class herself. Elaine, the director of the senior citizens center, and the lady's middle-aged son talked to her as if they were coaxing a child into the hospital. In the end, the elderly mother agreed to observe the class for the time being, and so she took a seat. As soon as Elaine and the lady's son left the room, most members of the class who had waited impatiently started speaking to her at the same time. The lady was from Hungary and seemed to be unable to speak English fluently, as Elaine had explained. She sat with a look of confusion upon hearing the ladies' welcomes fill the room.

When I began to cut the fabric for the dress for Muriel's baby doll at the table by the window, Rose, who had been sitting with her back to me, suddenly stood up and went over to the Hungarian lady. Rose weakly smiled at the lady and then touched her shoulder. Crouching a little, she began speaking eagerly to the timid-looking lady. As the ladies' welcome speeches came to an end, I went back to my work and started to pin two pieces of fabric together, listening to the words of Rose behind me. The voice sounded beautiful but painful. The previous week Rose's brother and her favorite nephew had died. Even if she might have been the most suitable person for soothing the lonely newcomer, I thought, she didn't have to put on a good show. There hadn't been enough time to heal her sadness yet. When I turned around, however, I saw Rose beaming. If I had been an American woman, I wouldn't have hesitated to hug her saying, "Oh, Rose, how great you are! I am proud of you," just as she used to do for me. I, a shy woman, could do nothing but smile at her with all my heart. I realized that there were some customs that are hard to change no matter what the circumstances are. Even if I wouldn't be able to have her comprehend how much I thought of her, this was my way. However, Rose quietly smiled back and nodded twice as if she understood what I thought. In the room filled with women chatting, I felt at that moment as if Rose and I stood in a special, still place, facing each other.

Other members of the class also were people who might have experienced many sorrows in their long lives. Nevertheless, they were always cheerful and genuine about their feelings. They were especially open to newcomers. I, too, was a Japanese volunteer who had been welcomed warmly to this Senior Citizens Center two years earlier. The newcomer that day didn't have the shape of a cherub with wings, or a bow and arrow like the ones you see in pictures, but in my mind she had been as helpful as a Cupid. She made the class lively, Rose regain her confidence, and me believe that the differences between two cultures didn't matter as long as we trusted in each other. All of these, however, originated in the most admirable characteristic that Americans have: hospitality. The class was full of love that day.

These accounts were from the doll-making class at the Senior Citizens Center, Teaneck, New Jersey, before Christmas of 1989. Then the class welcomed newcomers Eileen, Ruth, Evelyn, and two ladies named Hazel. A new instructor, Yoko, also joined us.

㉔ *At the Risk of One's Life*

AMERICANS, generally speaking, seem to be a people who essentially love freedom. So far as I saw during my five-year stay in America, they were apt to do what they liked in any given situation, even while they were driving. It seemed that they were willing to carry out most of their routines, except for going to the bathroom and to bed, at the risk of their lives.

One chilly afternoon in December 1989, on the way back home from Manhattan to Fort Lee, New Jersey, I took a New Jersey Transit bus from the Port Authority Bus Terminal on 42nd Street. I sat down on the front seat on the right side. The bus left soon and passed through the Lincoln Tunnel. When the bus came to a hill, the driver let go of the wheel with his left hand which had also been holding a wad of money that passengers had paid. He then removed his right hand from the steering wheel too. As I looked on in disbelief, he held the wad again tightly with his hands and began to count the bills. In Japan I had never seen such a terrible scene, bus drivers doing another job without holding the steering wheel while they were driving. The lives of about forty passengers—including my own—should have been in his hands, but the money was there instead. The bus kept moving ahead. I fixed my eyes on the daredevil driver's fingers, which were leisurely turning over the bills one by one instead of holding the steering wheel. Eventually I could see that he hadn't let go of the steering completely: He was using his elbows to steer the bus! He glanced ahead sometimes, too, but none of these things reassured me. "One, two, three . . . thirty-eight," holding my breath I counted the number of bills with him. I prayed he would finish his performance as soon as possible—and then he started recounting the money to make sure, like a slow bank clerk! What's more, no American passengers around me seemed to care about the driver's risky behavior. Almost unintentionally I turned to get a look at the oldest man in the group. I expected that elderly people, in general, should be expert in dissuading people from doing wrong, as I used to rely on my older brothers and sisters to take care of problems for me. The ruddy-faced old man noticed me and smiled and then nodded as if he fully understood what I wanted to ask him. Even if there were some differences between Americans and Japanese, I thought at that moment, we could have mutual understanding as human beings. I felt relieved at last. "Hey!" the old man bravely said to the driver on behalf of all the rest of the passengers, "Hey, you made money, did you?"

On a bright morning in May 1990, near the middle of the downhill part of Fort Lee Road in New Jersey, my car was in a traffic jam because of some construction work. As cars slowed down on the slope, I could see the smoke of a cigarette rising from the slightly open rooftop window of the car ahead of me. The sunlight streamed through the gentle green leaves over the road. When I opened the windows, a fragrant breeze blew across my face. Some cars honked their horns. Most of the drivers passing by seemed to become irritated. I, too, became nervous in this irregular situation. When my car and the one behind mine proceeded to a level part of the road, I looked in my rearview mirror and saw a handsome man smiling and holding something brown. He seemed to be playing a guitar while driving.

After the experience with the bus driver, I wasn't surprised to see a driver doing something else while he was driving. However, I got confused again when I saw that he was using neither his elbows nor the lower part of his arms to steer his car. In my mirror he seemed to be singing a song accompanying himself on a guitar, as if he were enjoying the most beautiful season of the year. He opened the window as he found an audience before him, not under a shady tree but in a traffic jam. Afraid of being involved in an accident, I couldn't enjoy listening to him. The palms of my hands started perspiring as I worried about this crazy man colliding with my car. When we approached the construction site, I thought he would surely be warned against such stupid behavior by those who were directing the traffic around there. His voice was so beautiful that it made me feel sad. Cars proceeded at a snail's pace to where the work was being done. His song and the sound of the guitar aroused curiosity from the men at work along the street. There was a policeman there just as I had thought. With a look of keen interest he approached the car behind mine in a more authoritative manner than I had expected. What I heard as I left, however, was the officer saying in a loud voice to the musician, "Fantastic!"

On a depressing morning in June 1991, at home in Japan, I found an article titled "California Commuters Find Ways to Pass the Time" in *The Japan Times*.* The article was about ways to overcome the boredom of long drives, citing many examples including a report from Peter O'Rourke, Director of the California Office of Traffic Safety. It opened my eyes to the fact that my two previous experiences in the United States had been matters of everyday occurrence for Americans. According to the article, people shave, put on makeup, drink coffee, eat breakfast, read the paper, talk on the car phone, play musical instruments using their knees to steer the car, exercise by pushing their body against their seat belt or working their face and neck muscles by making grimaces, floss their teeth, and so on—all while they are driving their cars! Even though I still thought that such behavior invited traffic accidents, I couldn't help but be impressed with the Americans' free way of thinking.

In the year and a half since I returned to Japan, I have never seen such breath-taking scenes like the ones I saw in the United States. At most, bus drivers in Japan will po-

* *The Japan Times,* June 27, 1991.

litely raise their right hand with a white glove to the forehead to greet another bus driver as their two buses pass each other. Consequently, I can comfortably doze in the bus seat. Yet, because I have been influenced by the risky way Americans drive, the safety of the Japanese way now sometimes bores me to death.

25 *Wings*

ON JUNE 22, 1989, during the fifth year of our family's sojourn in Fort Lee, our older son was graduated from Fort Lee High School a year early, as an accelerated student.

The reason he rushed was that he wanted to go back to Japan and start his college life with his old Japanese friends beginning in April 1990. In Japan, school begins in April, and he would have been a senior at a high school there from April 1989 to March 1990. He liked the United States, but I think he was unable to bring himself to accept social problems such as drugs and teen pregnancy, which he heard about and saw around him in his high school.

The American school system complied with the Japanese boy's personal request. My husband had some interviews with the high school guidance counselor to help accomplish our son's hope of acceleration. Consequently, our son became very busy studying during those three years. To fulfill the requirements at Dwight-Englewood summer school, he took additional credits in geometry in 1987 and in pre-calculus in 1988, while I was his chauffeur. When he took the TOEFL,* my husband took him to the test centers.

During his school years, our older son led a regular life. He left home at 7:55 A.M. and returned at 3:05 P.M. Unlike in our hometown in Japan, no shops that teenagers liked were along the road from home to school. He mostly seemed to walk under the big trees along Linwood Avenue and Lincoln Avenue as he watched squirrels holding acorns. Though he had passed the E.S.L. and bilingual class at the end of ninth grade, in 1987, he still had a few language problems. Even in doing homework, he had to take more time than his American classmates did, but he no longer needed his father's help for his daily work. He went to bed later than we did and got up before we did sometimes. He often looked pale, but he was happy at the same time because the teachers recognized his achievements. They kept on encouraging this foreign boy who was coping with difficulties alone. He came to respect some teachers, not only as teachers but also as ladies and gentlemen. In each high school class he always was allowed to concentrate all his energy on a problem, and he made efforts to create his own solutions. This was one of the splendid things he learned from American education. He also loved the camera club and became its vice president when he was in eleventh grade. All these were just because he

* Test of English as a Foreign Language.

had wanted with all his heart to get back to Japan earlier. Because of this desire, however, his second American life turned out to be busy but at the same time became richer and more promising than he had expected. In the end, he was chosen to be a member of the National Honor Society. His face was as bright as the gold-colored shawl hanging from his shoulders at the graduation ceremony.

At the high school, not only the regular class teachers but also the bilingual teacher and the guidance counselors supported him. He made good friends and met a kind crossing guard, as well. Also, he met a lady who gave him encouragement from across the lunch counter every day. Mrs. Irene Guidera, who was a high school cafeteria worker as well as a nice next-door neighbor, also made a point of inviting our sons over when the Halloween candies were ready.

On June 24, 1989, two days after the graduation ceremony, our older son completed his stay of four years and two months in Fort Lee and returned alone to Japan from John F. Kennedy Airport. Since my husband's assignment in New York wasn't finished, we asked our son's grandmother to take care of him in Japan until the rest of us got back home. That day, Kyosuke, whose wings had been clipped in the beginning of his American life because of the language problem, seemed to spread those wings at the airport. My husband and I saw him off and watched until the airplane had vanished into the blue sky with a load roar.

In the fall, as a returning student, he took several university entrance examinations in Tokyo and was accepted by three universities. He chose the law department at Keio University and started his college life the next April.

26 *Silence and Noise*

IT WAS still early morning, and the large terminal of Gatwick Airport in Britain was cool and quiet. In the summer of 1990, our family spent two days in London on the way back to Japan after a five-year stay in the United States. Stifling our yawns brought on by jet lag, we rode the escalator from the terminal to customs. Carrying my big suitcases I assumed that at this moment near the exit there would be many Britons who would noisily welcome new arrivals, as Americans do. I presumed that Westerners in general—Americans, British, French—would behave similarly. When our family got to the exit, however, we stood looking at one another. Even though many people had been waiting for the arrivals to come out, the atmosphere was so quiet it woke us up from our jet lag. The people around us were tall and neatly dressed. Some just stood, others stood with arms folded, and many smiled but said nothing. Soon, each of them began to beam with delight and wave their arms as they found familiar faces among the arrivals. As they approached, they shook hands, hugged, kissed, and whispered to each other. Their behavior looked so smooth and beautiful. It was as if they were acting according to some form of etiquette or ceremony. Yet they seemed to be reserved and not as open as I had expected. This scene was a surprising contrast with what I had seen in the United States.

In the summer of 1988, the fourth summer of our American life, our family returned to New York from a two-week vacation in Japan. Around the exit at the arrival terminal of John F. Kennedy Airport, we saw many people who had waited to welcome the arriving passengers. As soon as the lines of new arrivals started coming out, the people who were waiting, most of whom were big and wore T-shirts and shorts, began to cheer, clap their hands, whistle, and call out loudly the names of friends and family. Although the welcome was not for us, it was for a young group who had shared the flight with us on Japan Air Lines. Beaming with delight the two groups shook hands strongly, as if two trains had connected. They hugged each other like football players clashing. They kissed each other as quickly as a stamp is canceled by a post office clerk. As I watched the scene I couldn't help but think of how many wonderful ways people express themselves. The scene was neither polished nor calm, but the energetic, lively, and free atmosphere was enough to make me believe the fact that America had welcomed newcomers from all over the world in this most generous way.

The silence among the gentle British people had awakened such memories of my life in America, where I had been only seven hours earlier. As our family left the terminal we were welcomed by England's fresh air and showered by her mild morning sunlight. It was a truly different Western world.

27 *A Long-awaited Opportunity*

FROM GATWICK Airport our family took a taxi and headed for the hotel in London. It was about seven o'clock in the morning. The taxi drove along a narrow, crooked, and empty road between gently sloping green hills. The peaceful view of the road completely fascinated us because for the past five years we had been used to America's dynamic vistas of wide roads that continued as far as the eye could see. At such a memorable moment, however, all of us were quiet because we missed our older son who had left by himself for Japan a year ago. In the soft morning sunlight, the scattered trees cast round shadows on the hills where flocks of sheep grazed. The land had a gentle slope to it, and through the slightly open window of the taxi, a breeze came in and comforted me.

The taxi driver broke the silence blowing his nose. He then began to speak through his nose. "The grass looks almost brown because we haven't had much rain yet this summer." Turning his head to the right and left, he repeated the words "brown" and "dry" as if he were driving us through the Sahara.

In my mind's eye, however, it was the pastoral English scene I had longed for since I had learned English poetry in my college days. For me this was the country of the great poets such as Keats, Browning, and Wordsworth. In such a quiet place, they might have been prone to recollection, considering life for hours in the gentle breeze.

The driver asked my husband what kind of plans we had for our short stay in London, but I continued to think of the poets. They had unstintingly put their heart and soul into their work and had created great poems. It might have been because God blessed England by giving her such a gentle climate which produced neither a tundra nor a desert under the burning sun. If I could savor one of my favorite poems before we passed through the farmland, I thought, this drive would be the height of happiness for me. The air might not be the same as those poets had breathed in the nineteenth century, but I wanted to share something with them. I took a deep breath of the cool air.

The driver sneezed. Then, while trying to turn around and look at us with a vulgar smile on his face, he began urging us to take a sightseeing tour of London at the price he was offering.

A famous poem of Robert Browning's occurred to me. Unlike the season in the poem, it was summer, however. I thought that the poem would serve as a reminder of this beautifully green, pastoral scenery forever.

> The year's at the spring
> And day's at the morn;
> Morning's at seven;
> The hillside's dew-pearled;
> The lark's on the wing;
> The snail's on the thorn:
> God's in his heaven—
> All's right with the world.
>
> (Song from *Pippa Passes*)

When I recall this poem in Japan, however, the English pastoral scenery is dry and brown. In addition, the driver's nasal voice rings in my ears and his vulgar smiling face closes in on me.

28 *Regarding Cabs*

OUR FAMILY took a taxi at Narita Airport when we returned from the United States in the summer of 1990. It was extremely clean. The seats were covered with freshly laundered white cloth. The windows were shining. Neither litter nor mud was seen on the floor. A box of tissue paper had been put in the back window. I could even smell a floral fragrance. As I look back, this was the Japanese standard. However, I had not lived in Japan for more than five years, and it seemed as if I were a tourist from the United States. The cleanliness of the taxi reminded me of contrasting experiences taking yellow cabs in the United States.

Once I rode in a remarkably messy yellow cab. The seats were stained. The windows were cloudy. Inside, both the floor and seats were littered with smashed, empty Coke cans, hamburger wrappers, and several other pieces of paper. The young driver, who looked like a poet, got out of the cab when he saw me hesitate to get in. If he were a Japanese taxi driver, he would say, "Sorry. I'll clean that up right now, ma'am," and would take out a broom and a dustpan from the trunk. However, it came as a refreshing surprise to see the American driver clean up the mess. He said, "It's a beautiful day, isn't it?" and pushed the litter into the far corner of the floor with his right foot. A minute later, I was sitting on the seat worrying that the stains on it would get on my skirt, and I was kicking a smashed Coke can as it kept rolling back toward me.

When I saw the meter of the Japanese taxi from Narita Airport start to run, I was sure that I had returned to Japan. I remembered that I didn't have to tip any driver in Japan. In the United States, trying not to pay more than the fare plus a fifteen-percent tip, I was always busy calculating mentally and watching the meter as my destination approached. I once miscalculated and gave the driver too big a tip. I understood too late why he turned so cordially to shake hands immediately after he took the money.

In the Japanese taxi, our family could hear unfamiliar Japanese love songs on the radio. The middle-aged driver, who appeared to be proud of his profession as a taxi driver, wore a white shirt with a tie, navy blue trousers, a pair of white gloves, and a cap with a white, cloth cover on it. He seemed to have worked for the taxi company for many years. He was very restrained and said nothing more than "Certainly, sir" when my husband told him our destination. This stiff behavior caused me to recall American drivers who had given the impression of being quite relaxed.

One summer day in America, I saw a young driver who was wearing sunglasses, a T-shirt, shorts, and sandals as if he had just come from the beach. While driving, he constantly shook his head listening to rock music on the radio. When there was a traffic jam, he didn't hesitate to say things like "Damn you!" and "Go to hell!" Many American drivers, in general, seemed to be working for the cab company temporarily. Young drivers especially might have been making money for some big goal in the future.

As time passed in Japan, I came to realize that there were various kinds of Japanese taxi drivers. Once I saw a driver throw cigarette butts out of the taxi window. No driver refused a tip if he was offered one. Some drivers yelled "*Konoyaro!*" (roughly translated, "You son of a bitch!") at each other when there was a traffic jam, too.

When I was suspicious of a Japanese driver although he talked to me kindly, I remembered that I had been moved almost to tears by an American driver's friendly encouragement at the beginning of my life in America. I had called a taxi from Fort Lee's Babe's Cab Company, calling from the Driver Testing Center in Lodi. I sat in the corner of the rear seat of the cab, upset and withdrawn like a clam, after failing the road test. When the cab arrived at my house, the driver, who looked to be in his early sixties, unexpectedly started to encourage me to practice driving some more. I was surprised to hear him speaking so sincerely to a stranger, but his words comforted me so much I was encouraged to try again.

Generally speaking, the experiences we have when living abroad wake us up. I learned a lot about my home country and my host country, from such small details as a dirty taxi cab. It seemed that the more trifling the matter was, the more it revealed the true character of the society.

29 *Driving*

ONE OF the memorable things about my life in America from 1985 to 1990 was that I drove a car.

We moved to Fort Lee, New Jersey, in the spring of 1985 because of my husband's new assignment in New York. Unlike Japan, the United States seemed too large to carry out the daily routine without driving a car. My husband already had a driver's license, but all my life I had never imagined getting one. Because we didn't have a car for the first several days, we walked around town as we settled into our new life. Soon my big denim shoulder-bag which I had brought from Japan was torn from carrying such heavy items as milk, cooking oil, and canned foods. In ten days I had sore feet. In two weeks I started thinking about getting a driver's license after hearing from my Japanese friend who had already gotten one in New Jersey. Then I began noticing people who drove their cars everywhere. Every driver, from a racecar driver to an elderly woman who caused a traffic jam, looked great to me because they all had passed the difficult tests and were driving their car confidently. I took the written test once and the road test twice in Lodi, New Jersey. I got my license in September. I was thirty-nine.

I remember the first day I drove to the nearest supermarket by myself. I took detours because I was trying to turn left as little as possible. I parked my car in the space farthest away from the store entrance because no cars were parked around me. I bought nothing but bathroom tissue because I was on tenterhooks until I arrived back home safely.

Being safe took precedence over everything—especially in the beginning. I depended on a supernatural power; while looking at his framed photograph, I prayed to my father, who had died long ago, to protect me from having an accident. I forbade my two sons to fight in our car by telling them beforehand, "You will be unable to see your grandparents in Japan again if I cause an accident because I was distracted by your noise." The two boys turned pale. I also took slower city streets when someone asked me for a ride in my car; those who disliked my slow driving didn't ask me again. Most of all, I was anxious about speaking English if an accident happened. If I were badly hurt, however, I would be unable to speak even in Japanese, I realized. The area of the United States is twenty-five times the size of Japan, and it is mostly flat. Though I was not going to drive all over the United States, I resented the vast area of the country.

Gradually, however, driving came to be a part of my daily routine. I drove my sons to their weekend Japanese schools, summer schools, swimming school, the library, the pediatrician, the dentist, the orthodontist, the ophthalmologist, the dermatologist, their friends' houses, movie theaters, the skating rink, TOYS-R-US, and so on. I also drove my husband to the bus stop on chilly winter mornings.

I used our car for myself, too. I had time to go out, and, as long as I didn't give any serious thought to economic, ecological, and cultural matters, I didn't have to be inside my house until the time school was over. For instance, in the United States, I had less housework than in Japan: I was free from gardening because the gardener came to mow the grass once a week. In the early morning, I didn't have to put much laundry out in the sun because I had a big dryer. I didn't attend any memorial services because I had no Japanese relatives in the United States. Moreover, I didn't have the Japanese rainy season in June. The days of early summer in the northeast United States were beautiful.

While my husband worked at an office in New York's World Trade Center tower building and while the children went to Fort Lee's public schools, I made short work of doing the dishes and cleaning the house and then had my own time. I drove to the library, adult schools, shopping centers, and friends' houses. I started volunteering in Teaneck, New Jersey, as well. Roads were wide. Cities were completely equipped for driving. If I hadn't driven a car during my five-year stay, I would have missed seeing the spaciousness and richness of American life. I learned, too, that quick judgment and fast decisions were always required for safe driving. I thought the reason why American women in general looked self-assertive might be partly because they had been trained by driving. Although I earned nothing, I felt I was going out into the world. Yet I was fully aware of being a beginner at driving. I didn't run risks; I preferred local roads and never drove to Manhattan.

One day, however, an accident occurred. My father's

supernatural power which I had been depending on from my first day of driving wasn't perfect. He must have taken a nap in heaven once while his daughter was driving in Fort Lee. On that day in October 1988, my car was hit when I was proceeding into an intersection on a green light. Another car suddenly jumped out from the right. With a big crash my car was lifted a bit above the surface of the street and swung around. "This must be an accident!" The next moment, however, I neither thought of my family nor my country, Japan. I was quickly making English sentences about the traffic accident which my teacher, Elizabeth, had taught me in her class. Nobody was injured after all. However, both a wheel cover and a part of a fender of my car were scattered over the road, and the fender was run over by oncoming cars. Besides that, the two doors and the center support on the right side of my white Pontiac were crushed. The area around the left headlight of the car that hit mine was smashed, and pieces of broken glass were scattered about, too. I was upset but lucky in some ways. First, we two drivers didn't have to roar at each other the way some American drivers did, because the other person spoke less English than I did. Second, a red public works truck happened to pass by and a man in uniform swiftly helped us and went to report the accident to the police department a block away. Third, the police officer who arrived then listened carefully to my English as I explained what had happened. It took three weeks to repair my car. Insurance covered the $3,200 cost. After a while, I resumed driving. I was more cautious than before, but at the same time I became more at ease, as if I had passed the barrier of an entrance examination to be accepted by the United States. I felt sure I had become closer to American society.

Before I left the United States, I still had time to appreciate the abundant nature along the roads which extended for miles and miles. With all my heart I wanted to make good use of every moment. When I began to listen to music on the radio and the cassette player in my car, the landscape looked like a gorgeous opera stage. Although sometimes there was a song with no singers, the stage was as high as the sky, as deep as the horizon, as full-colored as nature, and I was admitted free. Once in early summer, at a traffic light on a hill I had a commanding view of a town colored fresh green as, fortunately, I was fascinated by a dynamic passage of Dvořák's Symphony No. 9, "From the New World." When every flower was in full bloom in the yards of the houses lining the streets, I drove my car slowly as I enjoyed Mozart. The melancholy section of Tchaikovsky's Violin Concerto seemed appropriate to the crooked uphill road bordered by trees colored with autumn tints. At that time, the upper part of my body unintentionally moved with the music as I sat behind the wheel. I felt as if I had the wealth of the world when the harmony of music and nature so inspired me.

Winter passed and our sixth spring in America came. I was informed that my husband's assignment in New York would be finished in a few months. The spring sky, pink magnolia trees, old houses, shops, schools, and traffic signs which I had been familiar with looked fresh through the windshield of my car. I embraced the finite days in a fond farewell. At the end of July 1990, my family said good-bye to our Pontiac.

30 *Friction*

"OF COURSE, the Japanese copied it." One day in a small fabric shop, the female clerk unexpectedly said this to me and pointed to a roll of European cloth on my right. She might have mistaken me as being from another Asian country. I had been fascinated by some fancy cloth imported from Japan, which was similar to the European-made material next to it.

"The show was beautiful but imitative, wasn't it?" a tall young woman said to her friend beside me after a show at Radio City Music Hall by the Japan girls' dancing team.

When my husband and I asked an auto repair shop to exchange regular tires for snow tires, in the office we could hear one elderly customer say to his friends while glancing at us, "Japanese stole the idea. . . ."

While I lived in the United States, I saw that not only hostile Congressmen in the media but also ordinary people often showed their annoyance with Japan. Even if the shop clerk had been unaware that Japan had had techniques for making traditional kimono fabrics for hundreds of years, it was not incorrect that Japan had learned many things from the Western world, as the others mentioned. But those Americans' ways of stating their opinions seemed to tell how much the Japanese irritated Americans. Economic friction between the two countries was increasing.

Around the latter half of 1980s, Japanese investors bought American properties one after another. In the fall of 1989, the fifth year of our family's American life, I heard the news that Japanese companies had purchased properties that were American symbols. Sony acquired Columbia Pictures Entertainment and soon Mitsubishi Estate Company agreed to pay for a fifty-one-percent share of the Rockefeller Group, including the famous Rockefeller Center. The news caused a stir. *Newsweek,* on October 9, 1989, carried the headline "Japan Invades Hollywood" on its front cover, and *TIME,* on November 13, 1989, ran an article under the headline of "Sure, We'll Take Manhattan." I didn't think that the Japanese companies' way was the best thing to do. Yet, in the sensational expressions of these two headlines, I saw the implication that Japanese were always vicious, while in fact these magazines just wanted to boost their sales.

Almost every day, TV and radio conveyed Americans' angry reactions to Japanese property investments. On a smaller scale, I couldn't imagine that a shopkeeper's neighbors, relatives, and friends would blame a Japanese customer if he or she bought an American product that was for sale in the shop. Of course, no one would ask the shopkeeper why he had sold the product. It all seemed strange. However, I did understand how Americans felt. *These* purchases were Americans' treasure, pride, and dream.

The Americans' reaction to the news reminded me of my personal experience two years earlier at the newly opened Japanese Gallery in the Metropolitan Museum of Art in New York in the spring of 1987. According to a Japanese monthly art magazine, the *Geijutsu Shincho* (July 1987), in 1979 the Japanese government had donated $1 million for the gallery. At the request of the museum in 1982, Japanese companies and citizens donated $3 million of a budget of $5.55 million. Surely the cooperation between Japanese and Americans to open the gallery sounded refreshing at a time when the tension was increasing between the two countries.

I visited the gallery in the summer of 1987 for the first time. When I stepped into the new gallery, the silence in the dimly lit space was overwhelming. A faint smell of wood and incense filled the air. A trickle of clean water could be heard near the center of the gallery. These gentle elements of Japanese culture calmed me at first after my two-year absence from Japan. The gallery was very authentically made and it reminded me of Japan's ancient capital, Kyoto. Many traditional Japanese works of art which had been created a thousand years ago or so were effectively displayed in the gallery. It was apparent that they were different from the European art that expressed passion and strong ego. They didn't look as dynamic as the art from other parts of the world, either. The artifacts from my small island country were simple, precise, elegant, and gorgeous in their own way. In them could be seen the aesthetic sense and responsibility of the ancestral Japanese artists. The opening of the gallery in New York really was a chance to help many people understand Japanese culture. But at that time I was not sure why so many beautiful treasures of Japan were owned by the museum. After my first visit, however, I learned from reading that some Japanese artwork had been taken away to the United States during the postwar era, after the United States had defeated Japan.

On my second visit, I carefully looked at the labels in the display cases and recognized that most of the exhibits in the gallery had been purchased from Americans and also had been donated by American collectors. To my surprise, the labels printed with Westerners' names humiliated and disillusioned me. I, who was born after the war, felt in retrospect the bitter experience of having been a loser. In the gallery I was left feeling as if all of the exhibits such as folding screens, armor, swords, vases, kimonos, lacquered boxes, and scrolls had been brutally carried off by GIs.

But my reaction was one-sided, too. The objects in the exhibits didn't originally belong to me. Besides, they might have been obtained through proper business deals with Japanese sellers who had needed the money to survive. Moreover, in a sense, the works of art had been saved in the confusion of the postwar era and fortunately were first shown openly in 1987, at last. Like many Americans who were angry because Japanese firms had bought America's soul, I could rationally understand why many Japanese works of art had been taken but I wasn't able to accept it emotionally at that time.

When I reflected upon Japan's conduct during the war years, and when I thought of myself being born in China in 1946, I felt guilty. However, Americans' anger toward

Japanese and my disappointment with Americans made me keenly aware that nobody liked to have a symbol of their country's culture taken over.

Since I had come to the United States in 1985, there was something that had been worrying me. It was my doubt that Americans knew very much about Japan. In the United States, there was too little information about the real, contemporary Japan. Even if there was some information, it was not always true. In many American movies, the barbaric aspects of Japan were exaggerated. In TV dramas that satirized Japan, actors mostly spoke in strange Japanese. In a social studies textbook used in the 1980s for middle school students, a picture of a Japanese family was mistaken for a family from another Asian country. Once, I saw an American who believed that Japan had had little culture before Commodore Matthew C. Perry of the United States Navy arrived and anchored his fleet of four men-of-war ships off Uraga at the mouth of Tokyo Bay in 1853.

As long as these mysterious images of Japan reminded Americans of my country being unfair in terms of trading with the United States, Americans might be unwilling to trust Japan. If I were a member of the U.S. Congress who had judged Japan on the basis of this stereotypical information, I wouldn't respect Japan as an independent country at first; I would be sure that I could win more votes in the United States when I put pressure on Japan, and then I would become irritated and complain about Japan's slow response to a reasonable proposal the United States had made. The cause of the current friction between the two countries might have been not only economic policy but also a lack of communication.

Japan was, however, responsible for some Americans' ignorance of Japan. Due to the nation's inferiority complex, its poverty, and its being absorbed in the task of collecting new information from advanced countries to rebuild itself after the war, Japan had been remiss about sending accurate information to the United States and to other countries. What Japan kept silent about for a long time, in other words, might have meant that it had presented its negative image not only to the United States but to the world. Besides, it might have caused many Western journalists to produce this distorted image of Japan. Many unpleasant images might have been changed if Japan had really communicated with the world.

If I were a member of the U.S. Congress who had a close friend who was a member of the Japanese National Diet, I would respect Japan as an independent country, try to gain popularity by using my political ability without "bashing" Japan, go to Japan and walk its crowded streets with my Japanese friend, checking to see how many American products were on sale. That night, I would stay in a small Japanese-style guest room in my friend's small house—not in a hotel. Lying in the short futon on the tatami, looking at the natural pattern of the wooden ceiling, I would think that the U.S. Congress should remake their proposals after considering the modest Japanese lifestyle I had found unexpectedly.

Probably because when I was growing up I heard that the U.S. Occupation forces unstintingly had helped poor

Japanese in the postwar era, and also because I grew up seeing American TV dramas and movies since the 1960s, for me, America had been a place I had admired too much to be able to see its reality.

From 1974 to 1975 and from 1985 to 1990, with my family I had a chance to see the real America. The America I saw was a really big country which had vast land, abundant natural resources, a strong military force, and people who had come from all over the world. Therefore, the problems it seemed to have were more varied than those of other countries. It seemed to have many suffering people in obscure corners of society, as well. Besides that, there seemed to be people who painfully remembered the war against Japan, as a great many people in other countries did too.

The America I saw, moreover, was full of charm. It was an open society, and the people were willing to realize their democratic ideal. America also had kindness and playfulness—so much so that it injected a new spark of life into my daily routine. Especially the ordinary Americans I met were quite friendly. One lady loved *ikebana,* the Japanese traditional art of arranging cut flowers, and she used to welcome my family to her home with her beautiful *ikebana.* Others were interested in writing haiku in English and liked the simple Japanese way of expression. Some had learned the Japanese language and understood how people went through hardships using a second language while living abroad. They had been able to see Japan through their own eyes and had never been influenced by any biased information.

While I lived in the United States, there was much unpleasant news between the two countries. At the same time, however, there was much good news at the grassroots level between Americans and Japanese. My second stay in the United States—five years, three months, and sixteen days—was witness to that.

Yuko Koyano was born in China in 1946 and grew up in Japan. She studied English at the junior college of Kyoto Women's University. From 1974 to 1975 and from 1985 to 1990, she and her family lived in the United States. She now resides in Funabashi City, Chiba Prefecture, Japan, with her husband and two sons and her mother-in-law.